MATCH OF THE DAY
ANNUAL 2017

This book belongs to: _____

_____ Age: _____

My favourite team is: _____

My favourite player is: _____

My highlight of 2016 was: _____

_____

WELCOME!

WOW, WHAT A YEAR!

It's been one of the most incredible 12 months in football history. Luckily for you, we've crammed all the highs (and some of the lows) into this year's Match Of The Day annual. So make yourself comfy and happy reading!

SPROUT FREE ZONE!

2016 THE YEAR IN BRIEF
WITH LUIS SUAREZ'S TEETH

Leicester shocked the world by winning the Premier League title – and Riyad Mahrez was PFA Player Of The Year!

Louis Van Gaal waved goodbye to Man. United and English footy by winning the FA Cup!

WHAT'S INSIDE YOUR MOTD ANNUAL?

P6
30 years of Lionel Messi!

P16
Every club's biggest ever signing!

P28
Who is the new Ronaldo?

P41
Is he the best Prem striker of all time?

P51
The epic story of Euro 2016!

THIS IS THE SENSATIONAL STORY OF
EURO 2016
24 TEAMS · 51 MATCHES · 108 GOALS

FEATURING... 11 Viking warriors, 3 lousy lions, 1 Swansea reject, 1 giant moth, 1 ridiculous penalty shootout & much, much more...

P64
Paz & Ketch's football world tour!

P75
The total weirdness of football!

96
PAGES
OF THE BEST FOOTY FUN!

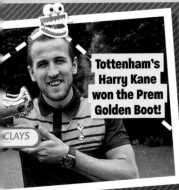

Tottenham's Harry Kane won the Prem Golden Boot!

Real Madrid were crowned European champions, beating city rivals Atletico in the Champions League final!

England lost to Iceland, Roy lost his job and Portugal won Euro 2016!

And Man. United smashed the world transfer record by signing Paul Pogba from Juventus for £89m!

30 YEARS OF MESSI

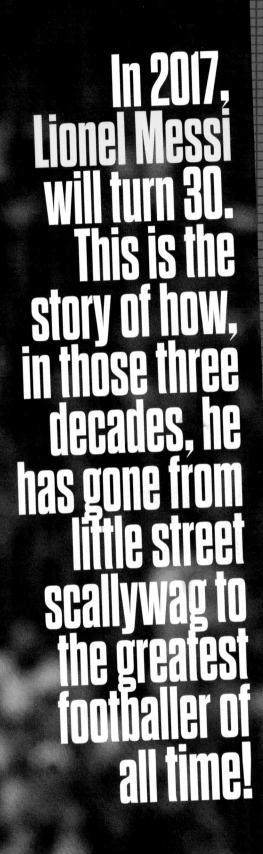

In 2017, Lionel Messi will turn 30. This is the story of how, in those three decades, he has gone from little street scallywag to the greatest footballer of all time!

▶▶▶ TURN OVER NOW!

THE STORY OF A LEGEND!

Leo, who became Barcelona's record goalscorer when he was just 24 years old, has bagged a staggering 376 goals in his last 373 games for the club!

1987 Leo was born in Rosario, central Argentina...

His dad Jorge was a steel factory manager and his mum Celia worked in a magnet workshop. Little Leo loved football and joined his local junior team Grandoli when he was just four years old. Leo was an instant success – his football journey had begun!

1993 £1,000

Messi then joined his favourite club Newell's Old Boys when he was six. In six seasons, he scored almost 500 goals as a member of The Machine Of '87 – the club's unstoppable youth team named after the year the players were born!

At the age of ten, Leo started having injections to help him grow because he was so small. But Messi's family and footy club struggled to pay the £1,000-per-month medical bill. They needed some help – enter Spanish giants Barcelona...

REXACH

2000 At 13, he left Argentina to move to Spain...

Barcelona scouts had heard about this wonderkid, and after a trial, first-team director Charly Rexach was so desperate to sign Messi he offered him a contract on a paper napkin! The club also agreed to pay the medical bills and to give Leo's dad a job. The family moved to Spain and Leo enrolled at the club's famous La Masia youth academy!

Leo, who made his Argentina debut in 2005 when he was just 18, has fired his country to the final of the 2014 World Cup and to THREE Copa America finals!

FROM WONDERKID TO MEGASTAR!

2005
2006
2007
2008
2009
2010
2011
2012
2013
2014
2015
2016

2004 Messi makes his Barca breakthrough...

Leo had become a key player for the Baby Dream Team, Barcelona's greatest-ever youth 11. During his first full season with the academy team, in 2002-03, Messi was top scorer with 36 goals in 30 games. Then in October 2004, he made his full La Liga debut, aged 17. A star was born!

5 MAGICAL MOMENTS!

2007
Scores an unbelievable solo goal against Getafe by dribbling from his own half!

2008
Little Leo wins a gold medal with Argentina at the Beijing Olympics!

2009
Scores in Barcelona's 2-0 Champions League final win over Man. United!

2010
Hits FOUR goals against Arsenal in a Champions League match in April!

2012
Smashes FIVE against Bayer Leverkusen in a UCL clash!

2016 13 seasons later, Messi is a legend...

He instantly became a Nou Camp hero – his mesmerising dribbling and astonishing goalscoring record fired Catalan giants Barca to an unprecedented period of success. He's won everything there is to win, has smashed every record in the book and now takes his place as the best of all time!

▶▶▶ TURN OVER NOW!

All stats correct up to 2 September 2016

LITTLE LIONEL'S BIG STATS

2004-16

BARCELONA

GAMES	GOALS	ASSISTS
535	456	181

ARGENTINA

GAMES	GOALS	ASSISTS
113	55	36

TOTAL

GAMES	GOALS	ASSISTS
648	511	217

WHY HE'S BEST EV

His speed of thought and speed of feet are unmatched in the history of football – and so are his stats...

Before Messi swaggered onto the scene, football's most impressive records were shared amongst the greats of the game. But like an all-conquering heavyweight boxer, the little Argentinian megastar has claimed pretty much all of the titles for himself. It truly is an astonishing achievement. All hail football's undisputed champion!

- Barcelona and La Liga all-time record goalscorer!

- Scored more goals for Argentina than any other player in history!

- Been named world player of the year a record FIVE times!

TROPHY CABINET

- 8 La Liga
- 4 Copa Del Rey
- 4 Champions League
- 7 Spanish Super Cup
- 3 European Super Cup
- 3 Club World Cup

SUITS YOU, SIR LEO!

People are so used to seeing Leo pick up the Ballon D'Or – he's got five of the little blighters now – that the big talking point is normally which wacky suit he's going to wear to the big bash. This crazy little number from 2013 is probably his best so far!

29

THE
ER!

MESSI'S SKILL CIRCLE
HOW HE RATES OUT OF TEN!

GOALSCORING

SPEED

DRIBBLING

CREATIVITY

HEADING

VISION

PASSING

FREE-KICKS

BORN Rosario, Argentina
DATE OF BIRTH 24 June, 1987 (age 29)
HEIGHT 5ft 7in
WEIGHT 10st 5lb
PREFERED FOOT Left

"He's a genius. Best ever by a distance in my lifetime!" **GARY LINEKER, MOTD PRESENTER**

HE'S MR CONSISTENT! Back in the 2012-13 season, Messi scored in an incredible 21 consecutive games – he actually netted 33 goals in that period. Boom!

Did you know? He scored 91 goals for club and country in 2011-12 – the most scored by a player in one season in the history of footy!

MESSI'S BARCELONA RECORD!

SEASON	GOALS
2004-05	1
2005-06	8
2006-07	17
2007-08	16
2008-09	38
2009-10	47
2010-11	53
2011-12	73
2012-13	60
2013-14	41
2014-15	58
2015-16	41

trophies won in 13 seasons at Barcelona!

FOOTY CHAT!

We imagine what goes on in players' group messages...

BALLERS ONLY
CR7, Suarez9, Gaz_Bale, Messi_10

Messi_10
Anyone see this pic of Ronny? #crybaby

CR7
Anyone see this one?

Messi_10 has left

Gaz_Bale
You've killed him there, C-Ron! LOL!

Suarez9

UNITED LADS
DareToZlatan, Mata_8, DeGea1, Wazza, PogBOOM, Schweinsteiger31

DareToZlatan
Ready to see some magic from Zlatan?

DeGea1
It's about time! Bring on the new season

DareToZlatan **removed** Schweinsteiger31

PogBOOM

DareToZlatan
There you go, Mata... you might get a game now!

Wazza
#greatbanter

Epic bantz done, smug face activated!

ARSENE'S ARMY 16-17

Arsene Wenger, Jamie_Vardy9, RealMorata, Higgy_Higuain, Lukaku10, Mahrez_26

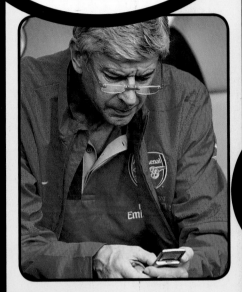

Arsene Wenger
created **Arsene's Army 16-17**

Jamie_Vardy9 left

RealMorata left

Higgy_Higuain left

Lukaku10 left

Mahrez_26 left

> **Arsene Wenger**
> Guys?

KLOPPO'S BOYZ

J_Milner, Cout10, Hendo, Clyney, Wiljn5ldum

> **J_Milner**
> What do you guys think of my new boots?

> **Hendo**
> Is that a joke, Milns?

> **Clyney**
> These are more like you bro

> **J_Milner**
> Okay, fair enough.

> **Cout10**
> #owned! Hahaha...
> Clyney 1 Milner 0

I was only trying to be a cool cat, guys!

EMOJI LOOKALIKES!

DELE ALLI

TOTTENHAM
20

RONALDO QUIZ!

How good is your C-Ron knowledge?

Q1 HOW OLD IS C-RON? 29, 31 or 32?

?

Q2 IN WHICH PORTUGUESE CITY WAS HE BORN?
Funchal or Lisbon?

ANSWER

Q3 AT WHICH TEAM DID HE START HIS PRO CAREER?
Porto or Sporting Lisbon?

ANSWER

Q4 IS HE RIGHT OR LEFT-FOOTED?

?

Q5 WORDSEARCH
Find the five words related to Cristiano to gain a point!

L	T	G	C	O	B	J	G	R
A	I	P	J	S	X	O	E	Z
G	C	C	N	X	A	N	O	C
U	Z	X	K	L	N	D	T	O
T	X	H	S	I	L	C	E	H
R	M	Z	W	A	P	L	L	B
O	T	G	N	E	A	H	B	Q
P	M	O	S	E	S	I	V	R
G	R	Y	R	H	D	Z	N	Q

GOALS
PORTUGAL
REAL
RONALDO
WINNER

Q6 TRUE OR FALSE?
Ronaldo's dad was the kit man for his team as a youngster!

ANSWER

Q7+8 GOALS GALORE
Which two superclubs has Ronaldo never scored against?

ANSWER   ANSWER

Q9 PRIZE FIGHTER! Which trophy has Ronaldo won the most?

FA CUP   COPA DEL REY

ANSWER

BALLON D'OR   EUROPEAN CHAMPIONSHIP

Q10 PITCH PERFECT!
Where does Ronaldo play home games for Real?

ANSWER

YOUR SCORE

/10

ANSWERS ON p92!

YOU PAID HOW MUCH?

Every Premier League club's record signing revealed. Here. Just for you. Enjoy!

ARSENAL

MESUT OZIL

£42.4m

From Real Madrid
September 2013
The man: Ozil, one of the world's top playmakers, had finished second in the La Liga assists chart behind Andres Iniesta but was forced to make way at Real for the incoming Gareth Bale!

What happened next? The German was an instant success at the Emirates, bagging 14 assists in his first campaign – he is now in his fourth season at Arsenal!

BOURNEMOUTH

JORDON IBE

£15m

From Liverpool
July 2016
The man: Four years after joining Liverpool from Wycombe, the 20-year-old winger had struggled to nail a first-team spot at Anfield – making just 12 Premier League starts last season!

What happens next? The England Under-21 winger will be hoping extra game time down on the south coast leads to a full international call-up in the future!

BURNLEY

£10.5m

JEFF HENDRICK

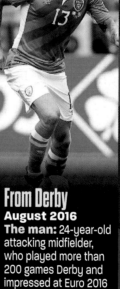

From Derby
August 2016
The man: 24-year-old attacking midfielder, who played more than 200 games Derby and impressed at Euro 2016 for Rep. Of Ireland!

What happens next? This will be Hendrick's first taste of Prem footy – he'll hope it isn't a short stay!

CHELSEA

FERNANDO TORRES

£50m

From Liverpool
January 2011
The man: Torres was in his fourth season at Liverpool and the Spain star was established as one of the world's greatest strikers!

What happened next? The move was a disaster for club and player – Torres took 13 games to get his first goal. He scored just 20 goals in 110 games before leaving for AC Milan. He's now at Atletico Madrid!

CRYSTAL PALACE
CHRISTIAN BENTEKE

From Liverpool
July 2016
The man: The 25-year-old striker found himself frozen out of the Liverpool starting line-up following Jurgen Klopp's arrival at Anfield – despite scoring for fun since moving to the the Prem in 2012!

What happens next? The big Belgian frontman will be hoping to recapture the form he showed during his three-year spell at Aston Villa, which prompted Liverpool to spend more than £32m on him back in July 2015!

£32m

HULL

£13m

RYAN MASON

From Tottenham
August 2016
The man: Mason was a regular in the Spurs midfield two seasons ago – but following the signing of Victor Wanyama he found himself down the pecking order at the Lane!
What happens next? Mason joins ex-Tottenham men Tom Huddlestone, Jake Livermore and Michael Dawson at the KCOM Stadium – and will be hoping regular first-team football helps him get back into the England squad!

LIVERPOOL
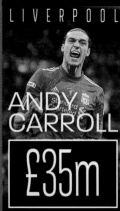
ANDY CARROLL

£35m

From Newcastle
January 2011
The man: The giant 22-year-old striker had scored 11 goals in 19 league games and he'd made his full England debut two months earlier!

What happened next? Carroll was signed to replace Chelsea-bound Fernando Torres, but he only managed six Prem goals before leaving for West Ham 18 months later!

MAN. CITY

£55m

KEVIN DE BRUYNE

From Wolfsburg
August 2015
The man: Kev had left Chelsea and just been named Player Of The Year in Germany!

What happened next? The 24-year-old scored 16 goals and assisted 12 goals in his first season in Manchester!

EVERTON

ROMELU LUKAKU

From Chelsea
July 2014
The man: The Belgian striker had just hit 16 goals in 33 games on loan at Everton – impressing then boss Roberto Martinez so much that the deal was made permanent!

What happened next? Rom continued his good form in front of goal, scoring 45 times over the next two seasons and having a huge £65m price tag slapped on his shoulders!

£28m

£29m

LEICESTER
ISLAM SLIMANI

From Sporting Lisbon
August 2016
The man: The 28-year-old Algeria striker, who was mega at the 2014 World Cup, has been the best striker in Portugal for the last two years and scored 27 goals last season!

What happens next? Slimani joins his Algerian team-mate Riyad Mahrez at the King Power – and will be hoping to replicate his countryman's success in the Premier League!

▶▶▶ **TURN OVER FOR MORE!**

MAN. UNITED

£89m

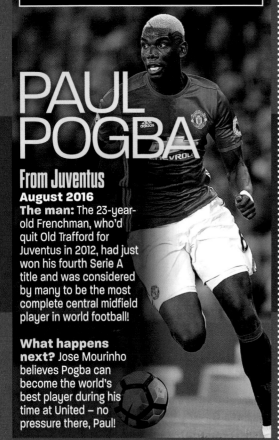

PAUL POGBA

From Juventus
August 2016
The man: The 23-year-old Frenchman, who'd quit Old Trafford for Juventus in 2012, had just won his fourth Serie A title and was considered by many to be the most complete central midfield player in world football!

What happens next? Jose Mourinho believes Pogba can become the world's best player during his time at United – no pressure there, Paul!

MIDDLESBROUGH

AFONSO ALVES

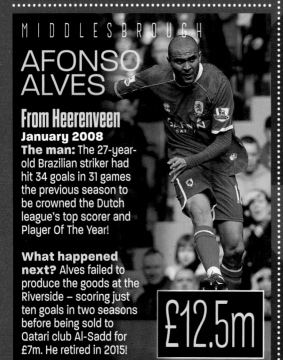

From Heerenveen
January 2008
The man: The 27-year-old Brazilian striker had hit 34 goals in 31 games the previous season to be crowned the Dutch league's top scorer and Player Of The Year!

What happened next? Alves failed to produce the goods at the Riverside – scoring just ten goals in two seasons before being sold to Qatari club Al-Sadd for £7m. He retired in 2015!

£12.5m

SOUTHAMPTON

£16m

SOFIANE BOUFAL

From Lille
August 2016
The man: The 23-year-old Morocco forward, being scouted by some of Europe's top clubs, had helped Lille to fifth place in Ligue 1 by scoring 11 goals!

What happens next? Saints fans will be hoping Boufal does better than previous record-singing Dani Osvaldo, who lasted just five months before being booted out after a training ground bust-up!

STOKE

£18.3m

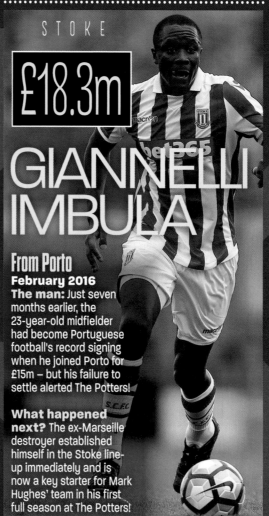

GIANNELLI IMBULA

From Porto
February 2016
The man: Just seven months earlier, the 23-year-old midfielder had become Portuguese football's record signing when he joined Porto for £15m – but his failure to settle alerted The Potters!

What happened next? The ex-Marseille destroyer established himself in the Stoke line-up immediately and is now a key starter for Mark Hughes' team in his first full season at The Potters!

£13.6m

SUNDERLAND

DIDIER N'DONG

From Lorient
August 2016
The man: The Gabon star only moved to Lorient 18 months ago from the Tunisian league – but his tough-tackling displays in midfield had caught the eyes of many scouts!

What happens next? David Moyes will be hoping N'Dong can make a similar impact to another unknown midfielder picked up from the French league – N'Golo Kante!

SWANSEA

BORJA BASTON

From Atletico Madrid

August 2016

The man: The Spanish striker hit 18 goals last season for Eibar in the Spanish top-flight, but was deemed surplus to requirements by Atletico boss Diego Simeone!

What happens next? Baston had five loan spells during his seven years at Atletico – hitting double figures in each of the last three seasons – and will be hoping to keep that up!

£15.5m

WATFORD

WEST BROM

£13m

NACER CHADLI

From Tottenham

August 2016

The man: The 27-year-old winger, who'd joined Spurs for £7m in 2013, had made 119 appearances for the club but found himself down the pecking order!

What happens next? The Belgian will be hoping for a better start at The Hawthorns than he had at Spurs – he only scored once in 24 games in his first season in the Prem!

TOTTENHAM

£30m

ERIK LAMELA

From Roma

August 2013

The man: With Gareth Bale expected to seal a big money move to Real Madrid, Tottenham earmarked the 21-year-old Argentinian winger as his long-term replacement!

What happened next? He played just nine times in his first season at White Hart Lane, but now in his fourth, Lamela has become a key player for Mauricio Pochettino!

£13m

ROBERTO PEREYRA

From Juventus

August 2016

The man: The attacking midfielder has spent the last two seasons at Juve, clocking up almost 50 Serie A games. He was also part of Argentina's 2015 Copa America squad!

What happens next? Struggled for game time last season – he'll be confident of nailing a first-team spot at Vicarage Road this campaign!

WEST HAM

£20.5m

ANDRE AYEW

From Swansea

August 2016

The man: The forward had joined Swansea on a free in the summer of 2015, after eight seasons in France. He hit 12 goals in what was to be his only season in South Wales!

What happens next? The pressure was on Ghana international Ayew to deliver the goals which will fire West Ham up the Premier League table, but he got injured on his Hammers debut!

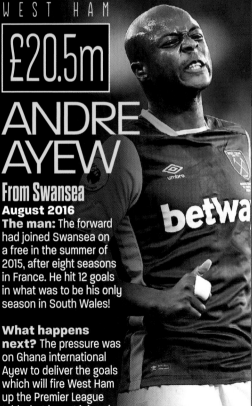

TOP 10 TYPES OF GOALS!

From first-time bangers to ferocious free-kicks, MOTD mag counts down the best ways to hit the net!

10

THE PENALTY

Putting the ball in the back of the net might seem easy from 12 yards, but it still requires wicked tekkers and nerves of steel. Our tip? Pick your spot early and focus on powerful yet controlled contact – oh, and top bins always looks sick!

....

THE MASTER: Eden Hazard
DIFFICULTY RATING: 4/10
WOW FACTOR: 🔥🔥🔥🔥🔥

9

THE FIRST-TIME STRIKE

To hit the ball without a first touch to set yourself requires real control and precision – otherwise it'll end up in the stands! Players often miss open goals when there's no time or space for a first touch, so to see one thunderbolt past the keeper will raise the roof!

....

THE MASTER:
Robert Lewandowski
DIFFICULTY RATING: 6/10
WOW FACTOR: 🔥🔥🔥🔥🔥

RECORD BREAKER! Lewandowski broke FOUR world records when he scored five in nine minutes against Wolfsburg in 2015!

▶▶▶ TURN OVER FOR MORE GOALS!

8

THE HEADER

No matter what type of header is scored, whether it's powerful, diving or cushioned, to put your neck on the line for your team has to be admired! When there are ten players all grappling for the ball in the box, it takes an impressive amount of strength to rise above the rest and power one home!

....

THE MASTER: Andy Carroll
DIFFICULTY RATING: 5/10
WOW FACTOR: 🔥🔥🔥🔥

7

THE ONE-ON-ONE

There's ten minutes left, you've beaten the defence and there's only the keeper to beat. He's off his line and spread his body to block the goal. You HAVE to score! See? It's nerve-wracking isn't it? That's why a calm slot into the bottom corner looks ace!

....

THE MASTER: Luis Suarez
DIFFICULTY RATING: 6/10   **WOW FACTOR:** 🔥🔥🔥🔥

6

THE TEAM GOAL

We all love tiki-taka, especially when it ends with a goal! Barcelona are the kings of this and often make 50 passes or more before hitting the net. It takes all 11 players to be on the same page!

....

THE MASTERS: Barcelona
DIFFICULTY RATING: 8/10
WOW FACTOR: 🔥🔥🔥🔥

5

THE LONG-RANGER

Goals from outside the box come in all shapes and sizes, and nothing looks more special than hitting one top corner from 30 yards – but it takes a lot of practice! Some of our favourite goals of all time have come from outside the box!

....

THE MASTER: Cristiano Ronaldo
DIFFICULTY RATING: 7/10
WOW FACTOR: 🔥🔥🔥🔥🔥

4

Payet is a beast with a dead ball!

THE FREE-KICK

Every player thinks they can score free-kicks, but few rarely do! Why? Because getting the ball up and over a five-man wall is harder than it looks! You need concentration and phenomenal technique to find the perfect balance of accuracy and power!

....

THE MASTER: Dimitri Payet
DIFFICULTY RATING: 7/10
WOW FACTOR: 🔥🔥🔥🔥🔥

▶▶▶ **TURN OVER FOR MORE GOALS!**

3

The keeper isn't stopping this!

THE FULL VOLLEY

When the ball is in the air, there's a lot to consider – the speed, the direction and the spin! That's why when a player connects with a volley and it crashes into the back of the net, it's pretty much always a contender for goal of the season!

THE MASTER: Wayne Rooney
DIFFICULTY RATING: 8/10
WOW FACTOR: 🔥🔥🔥🔥🔥

2

THE MAZY DRIBBLE & FINISH

Watching Lionel Messi nutmeg, side-step and send seven players in a spin before scoring yet another goal is probably one of the most enjoyable sights you'll see in football. Only one or two players in the world have the ability to do this – that's what makes it so amazing!

THE MASTER: Lionel Messi **DIFFICULTY RATING:** 9/10 **WOW FACTOR:** 🔥🔥🔥🔥🔥

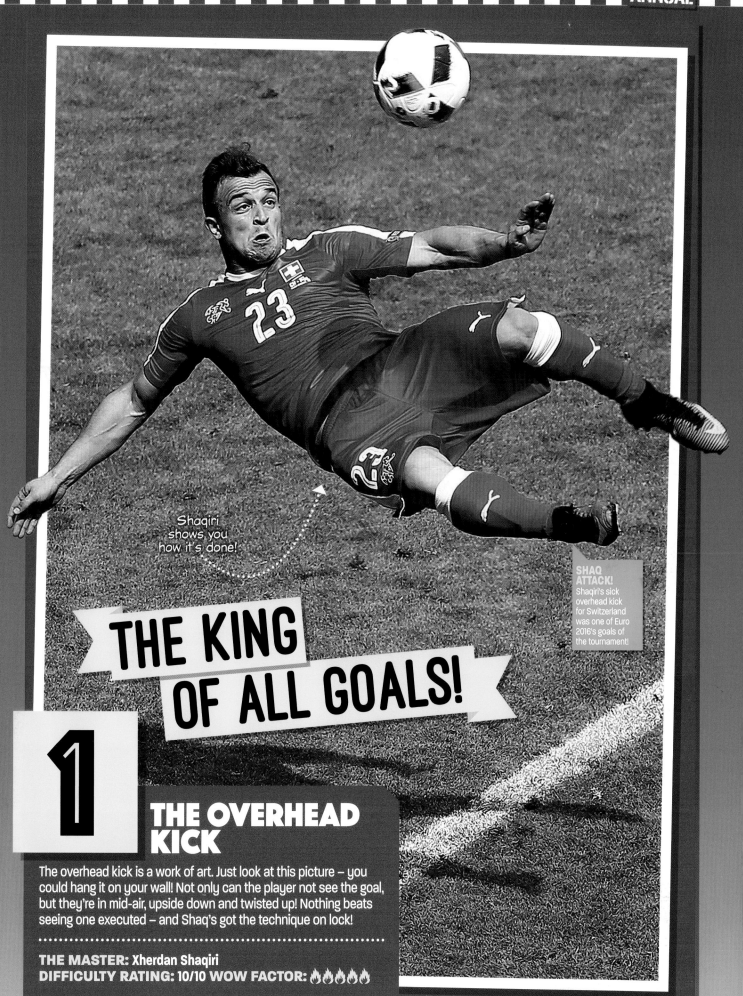

Shaqiri
shows you
how it's done!

SHAQ ATTACK! Shaqiri's sick overhead kick for Switzerland was one of Euro 2016's goals of the tournament!

THE KING OF ALL GOALS!

1

THE OVERHEAD KICK

The overhead kick is a work of art. Just look at this picture – you could hang it on your wall! Not only can the player not see the goal, but they're in mid-air, upside down and twisted up! Nothing beats seeing one executed – and Shaq's got the technique on lock!

THE MASTER: Xherdan Shaqiri
DIFFICULTY RATING: 10/10 **WOW FACTOR:** 🔥🔥🔥🔥🔥

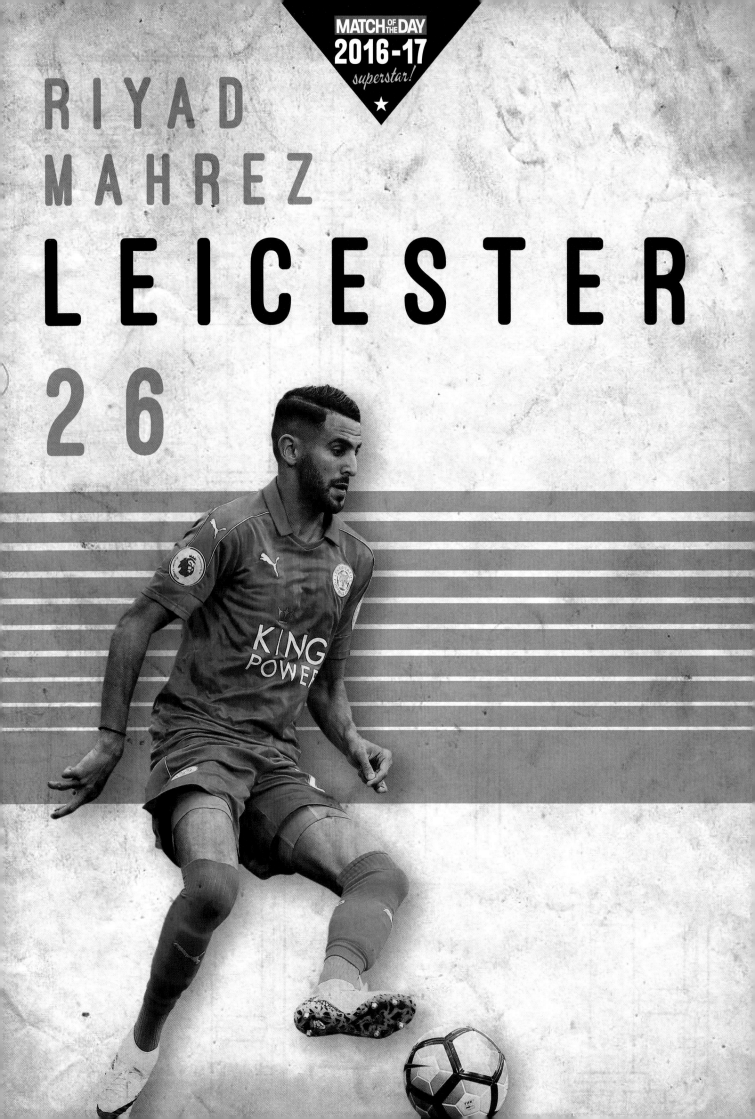

MATCH OF THE DAY
2016-17
superstar!

RIYAD
MAHREZ
LEICESTER
26

SPELLING TEST!

Guess the megastar by filling in the missing letters!

1 HENRIKH MK__I__AR__AN

2 __O__E

3 ILKAY GU__D____AN

4 DANIEL C__RV__J__L

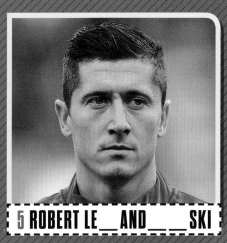

5 ROBERT LE__AND____SKI

6 ALEXIS __AN__HE__

7 SERGIO BU____UE__S

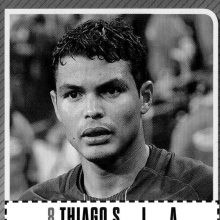

8 THIAGO S__L__A

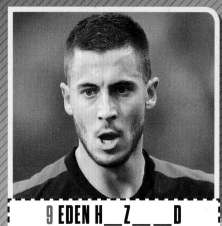

9 EDEN H__Z____D

WHICH FOOTY GCSE GRADE DID YOU GET?

1-3 = **C** Not a bad result, but if you revise a lot more you'll smash it next time!

4-6 = **B** Wow! What a great score – you really know your footballer spellings!

7-9 = **A** You've ACED it! Nothing gets past you when it comes to football – well done!

ANSWERS ON p92!

WHO IS
RONA

MOTD mag reveals the next big things set to rock footy!

HE NEXT LDO?

PLUS! MEET THE NEXT...

- **MESSI!**
- **IBRAHIMOVIC!**
- **NEYMAR!**
- **AGUERO!**

▶▶▶ TURN OVER NOW!

THE NEXT CRISTIANO RONALDO

Name: Goncalo Guedes
Club: Benfica
Country: Portugal
Age: 19

If Guedes is strutting his stuff in a Portugese Primeira Liga game, you can bet that scouts will be in the stands! He's one of Europe's most-wanted youngsters because of his dead-ball ability, tricky wing play and energy. Watch your back, C-Ron!

GUEDES WEARS Nike Mercurial Vapor XI

THE NEXT LIONEL MESSI

Name: Patrick Roberts
Club: Celtic On loan from Man. City
Country: England
Age: 19

Watch the Celtic dribble king play for five minutes and you'll wonder whether it's Leo himself! Barca boss Luis Enrique said Roberts is "set for a career at the very top" and we agree – especially with Pep Guardiola as his new gaffer back at City!

ROBERTS WEARS Adidas X 16+ Purechaos

THE NEXT
NEYMAR JR

THE NEXT
ZLATAN IBRAHIMOVIC

THE NEXT
SERGIO AGUERO

Name: Gabriel Jesus
Club: Palmeiras Joins Man. City in 2017
Country: Brazil
Age: 19

As his form for Brazil at the Olympics proved, the Palmeiras baller is the next big samba star! He's got the flicks, tricks and fancy footwork, plus he scored 19 goals in 31 games in 2015-16 while playing on the wing. It's no wonder Man. City have paid £27m to sign him!

Name: Dusan Vlahovic
Club: Partizan Belgrade
Country: Serbia
Age: 16

He's 6ft 2in, he scores goals and his surname ends with 'vic' – this one is nailed on! The 16-year-old Serbian forward is a big physical presence up front and shows flashes of brilliance even at his young age. Surely it won't be long before #DareToDusan becomes a thing!

Name: Sergio Diaz
Club: Real Madrid Castilla
Country: Paraguay
Age: 18

After making an impact in the Paraguayan league at just 15, Diaz made a move to Real Madrid, where he's currently in their B team. He's just like Aguero because of his sharp-shooting ability, his strong and stocky frame – and because his first name is Sergio!

JESUS WEARS Adidas X 16+ Purechaos

VLAHOVIC WEARS Nike Mercurial Superfly

DIAZ WEARS Nike Magista Obra II

BONKERS BADGES!

Just imagine if the top footy badges had a bit of a tickle to make them a little bit more suitable...

ARSENAL

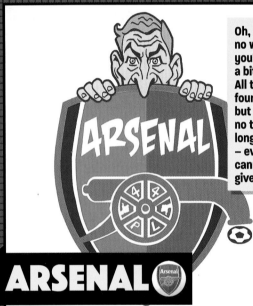

Oh, Arsene, no wonder you're looking a bit sheepish! All those top-four finishes, but it's now no title for 13 long, long years – even your cannon has given up hope!

BOURNEMOUTH

Come and get your cherries – lovely, juicy cherries! £2 for your cherries, folks! But how is this geezer expected to score if he's got cherries for eyes, eh?

BURNLEY

To be honest, Burnley's badge is bonkers anyway – but the introduction of some wasp spray, Sean Dyche, a ricocheting footy, a tweak to the club motto and an over-optimistic lion have done the business!

CHELSEA

Come on, how many blue lions have you ever seen in London? Exactly. That's why we've gone with the real Chelsea hero – moneybags owner Roman Abramovich! Now, does anyone know the Russian for 'put your tongue away'?

CRYSTAL PALACE

Those famous Eagles. The mightiest of the birds of prey, who'll gobble up anything and everything that comes before them. Er… that doesn't sound like the Crystal Palace we know! This podgy, doddery eagle is a bit more accurate!

EVERTON

Rapunzel, Rapunzel, let down your hair! Oh, it's not Rapunzel, it's 53-year-old Dutchman Ronald Koeman – and he seems to be celebrating the club's newfound wealth by throwing down some spare cash from his tower!

HULL

Beware the ferocious Tigers from Humberside! Okay, they're more like the toothless Tigers these days. That's why we've decided to leave this little fella wondering how he lost his bite!

LEICESTER

Cheer up, Claudio! You're a Prem champion – so in honour of that you can share the badge with the pesky fox. Oh, the fox has trumped, has he? All that eating from bins plays havoc with one's digestive system. Oops!

LIVERPOOL

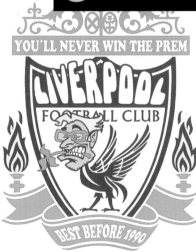

Can Kloppo get The Reds flying high in the Premier League and end 26 years of league misery on Merseyside? We'll soon find out, won't we?

Nothing says Man. City like a big chunk of gold. Simple. Actually, if that ship was made out of gold bars it'd be even more accurate. But would it still float? Who knows? Who cares?

MAN. CITY

MAN. UNITED

SUPERSTARS WANTED! MONEY NO PROBLEM!

Are you a superstar? Will you sell loads of shirts in the Far East? Will you cost a gazillion pounds in transfer fee and wages? Then you're perfect for United and their dream of world domination!

MIDDLESBROUGH

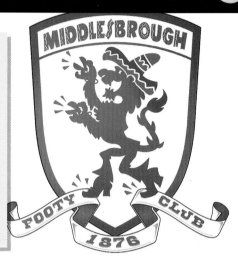

It's all gone a bit Viva Espana up at the Riverside, thanks to Aitor Karanka's Spanish revolution. The Boro lion is on board with his sombrero, castanets and flamenco gear! Now, where's that tapas?

STOKE

Oops! Has Pottermus been up to no good and foolishly found himself behind bars – or is it a great miscarriage of justice? Our motto has always been never trust a sky blue hippopotamus from north Staffordshire!

SOUTHAMPTON

Check out this crazy little fella. We've been thinking that if Peter Crouch was a football badge, he'd probably be this one. And he even used to play for The Saints. Party on, marching Saint, party on!

SUNDERLAND

Who on earth decided that Sunderland should have a couple of majestic black lions on their badge? Lions are the kings of the jungle, Sunderland are NOT the kings of the Prem. How about these bedraggled cats instead?

SWANSEA

Have you ever noticed that the Swansea swan actually looks like three toothy rats chasing after a snake? Well, you have now!

TOTTENHAM

So close last year, Spurs. So close to winning the Premier League before throwing it away and ending the 2015-16 season trophyless, leaving the fans a bit like this cockerel's ball – deflated!

WATFORD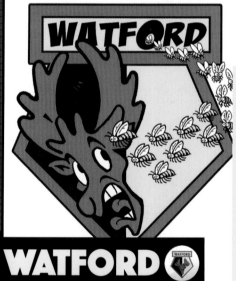

Quick question for Watford fans – if your nickname is The Hornets, why have you got a big, daft red deer on your badge? Those hornets aren't too happy about not being the centre of attention either. Aargh, gerroff!

We're not saying that West Ham are a one-man team, but, y'know...

WEST HAM

WEST BROM

This chirpy chappy loves nothing more than a morning warble on his favourite branch – but next door's hungry kitty is lurking. Fly away now, you birdbrain!

PIERRE-EMERICK AUBAMEYANG

BORUSSIA
DORTMUND 17

MATCH THE FACTS!

Connect these players with the footy statements below...

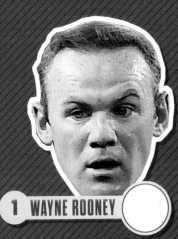

1 WAYNE ROONEY ◯

2 CRISTIANO RONALDO ◯

3 EDEN HAZARD ◯

4 SERGIO AGUERO ◯

5 MESUT OZIL ◯

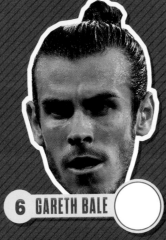

6 GARETH BALE ◯

7 PAUL POGBA ◯

8 PIERRE-EMERICK AUBAMEYANG ◯

A This fella has won the World Cup!

B He's won more than 70 caps for Belgium!

C This dude has won five Prem titles!

D He's played more than 100 games for Real Madrid!

E He made his Prem debut against Swansea!

F He won his first trophy with his country in July!

G He was named the 2015 African Footballer Of The Year!

H He joined his latest club for a whopping £89m!

WHICH ROUND DID YOU REACH?

1-3 = Ouch! You went out in the qualifying rounds. Hard luck!

4-6 = Good effort! Only a couple of mistakes – quarter-finals for you!

7-8 = Congratulations! You're a European footy knowledge champ!

ANSWERS ON p92!

THE 7 TYPES OF PLAYER IN EVERY SCHOOL TEAM!

1 THE ONE WHO IS A GLORY-HUNTING GOAL-HANGER!

It's hard to know whether to hate or love this little fella. He's the type of player who does absolutely nothing all game – diddly squat, zilch, nowt – but you can guarantee he'll pop up in the right place at the right time to poke home a later winner. He's the laziest player this side of Jupiter – but he gets all the glory. Grrr!

2 THE ONE WHO THINKS HE WILL MAKE IT AS A PRO!

He's had scouts watching him week in, week out, his uncle knows someone who knows someone at City and when he was at that summer soccer school a few years back, the coaches there told him he was the best 10-year-old they'd ever seen. Of course, it's all absolute rubbish – but who are we to kill the dude's big dream?

3 THE ONE WHO LOVES HIS HAIR!

He looks the real deal, this one. He's got the latest (and most expensive) boots, he can do keepy-ups all day long, loves a selfie and is always in front of the dressing-room mirror. But when the ball comes flying his way he'll duck, refuse to jump – do anything possible to protect his hair!

HIS HERO!

LIONEL MESSI,
Barcelona
& Argentina

4 THE ONE WHO IS AN ANNOYING BALL-HOGGER!

You may as well throw this kid his own ball and the rest of you play with another one – because you ain't gonna get many touches with Sir Dribbler on your team. His brain only has one setting – that's Head Down & Dribble Mode. He's actually pretty good – but he'd be a million times better if he passed the flamin' thing!

5 THE ONE WHO IS INSANELY QUICK!

Look, we all love a bit of tiki-taka and some cheeky one-touch footy – but with this kid up front just give it the old heave-ho, hit it long over the top and watch him outsprint the two lumbering centre-backs every single time. He's so quick he gets a gazillion chances every game – so it's a shame that his finishing is more miss than hit!

HIS HERO!

JAMIE VARDY
Leicester
& England

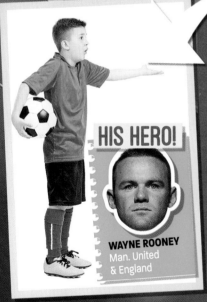

HIS HERO!

WAYNE ROONEY
Man. United
& England

6 THE ONE WHO NEVER STOPS MOANING!

Give it a rest, mate. From the moment the game kicks off to the second the full-time whistle goes, this dude does NOT shut up. He moans at the ref ("How was that not a foul?"), the linesman ("Are you blind? I was a mile onside!"), his team-mates ("You've got to make a run for me!") – even the grass is on the receiving end of his abuse ("Stupid pitch, it bobbled up!"). If only he was as good as he thinks he is, eh?

7 THE ONE WHO SHOOTS FROM EVERYWHERE!

Yes, we know you've scored some spectacular goals this season – but please, just once, can you lay it off or cross it because you are NOT going to score from there. Even if it's scientifically impossible to score, this fella will have a pop and watch his shot go sailing hundreds of miles wide of the post. Good one, mate!

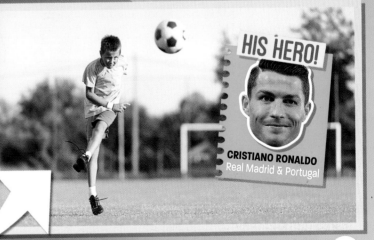

HIS HERO!

CRISTIANO RONALDO
Real Madrid & Portugal

REAL MADRID

11

GARETH BALE

10

SPOILER ALERT! Peter Crouch didn't make it!

BEST PREM STRIKERS... EVER!

▶▶▶ **TURN OVER NOW!**

10

ROBBIE FOWLER

162 PREM GOALS

You know you're doing something right when supporters call you God! One of the most natural finishers to ever appear in the Prem, Robbie was named PFA Young Player Of The Year twice – Wayne Rooney and Ryan Giggs are the only other two players to do that! He once scored a hat-trick against Arsenal in just 4 mins and 33 seconds, a record that stood for 20 years!

Best Prem goal? A missile at Old Trafford from a virtually impossible angle – even Prem ledge Peter Schmeichel couldn't get close to it!

SPICE BOY!

Robbie and his 1990s Liverpool team-mates had such a rep for partying they were nicknamed The Spice Boys after the famous girl-band!

9

IAN WRIGHT

113 PREM GOALS

Wrighty's career is a bit of a fairytale. He was picked up from non-league footy at the age of 22 and eventually signed for boyhood club Arsenal, where he went on to be their top scorer for six seasons! He also became The Gunners' all-time record scorer in 1997 and is still a firm fans favourite thanks to his lightning pace, fearless finishing and top banter!

Best Prem goal? Picked up a long hoof forward against Everton, juggled the ball on both feet to mug-off his marker then lobbed the keeper – class!

LIKE FATHER, LIKE SONS!

Wrighty's two sons Bradley and Shaun Wright-Phillips have both made successful footy careers – Shaun got more England caps than his dad!

8
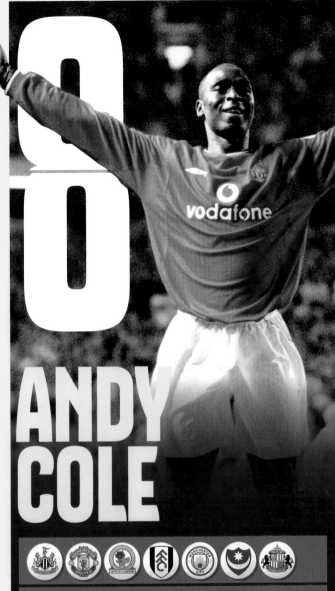

ANDY COLE

187 **PREM GOALS**

"When he gets the ball he scores a goal, Andy, Andy Cole!" So the song went – and it was true! Andy once scored 34 goals in one season for Newcastle – only MOTD man Alan Shearer ever managed as many in a single campaign! His 187 goals came for six different clubs, including Man. United where he hoovered up pretty much every honour in the game!

Best Prem goal? Andy's top effort was a 35-yard dipping volley at Anfield against Liverpool – not for Man. United but Blackburn!

COLEY'S CABINET! Andy's trophy haul is absolutely sick!

2   1   5   2

7

DIDIER DROGBA

104 **PREM GOALS**

Key goals in Drog's debut season helped Chelsea to their first Prem title, then he helped them win it all over again the following season! Drogba was the first African to score 100 Prem goals and he's also the only player to score in four separate FA Cup finals. A record of ten goals in ten finals and ten trophies won at club level make him the ultimate big-game player!

Best Prem goal? Chested the ball down with his back to goal, spun and hit a 30-yard volley over Tim Howard in the Everton goal!

KING DROG!

When he was subbed in his final game for Chelsea, Droba's team-mates carried him off the pitch like a king!

▶▶▶ TURN OVER NOW!

6

SERGIO AGUERO

105 PREM GOALS

Big goals often come in small sizes – Sergio Aguero is proof! For years defenders have tried to contain the 5ft 8in striker, who doesn't need an invitation to shoot! He loves wriggling between opposition players and letting off lightning bolt shots. His scoring rate in England is also ridiculous – only Alan Shearer reached 100 goals in fewer games!

Best Prem goal? His 94th-minute goal against QPR in 2012 won City the title and is possibly the most important Prem goal ever!

SCHOOLBOY SUPERSTAR!

Sergio made his professional debut for Independiente in Argentina aged just 15 – he reckons he'll also finish his career there!

5

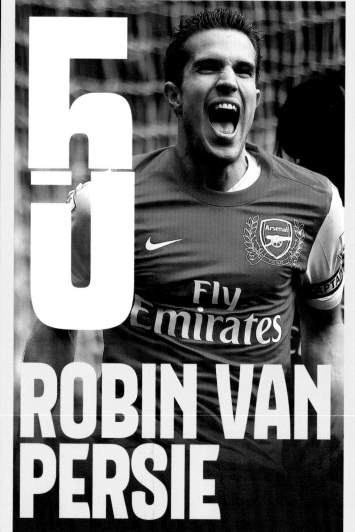

ROBIN VAN PERSIE

144 PREM GOALS

A deadly combo of power, grace, control and a sledge-hammer left foot has propelled RVP into the top five. He's done the bizzo for both Arsenal and Man. United, scoring every type of goal, from tap-ins to thunder-blasters and freekicks to flying headers. A totally devastating player on his day with a unique ability to introduce ball to a net!

Best Prem goal? An epic jaw-dropping volley against Aston Villa from a sick 50-yard Wazza pass – it was described as the goal of the century!

INJURY 'MARE!

Just think how many Prem goals he might have notched if he hadn't had so many injuries! He managed to play more than 30 league games in a season just twice!

4

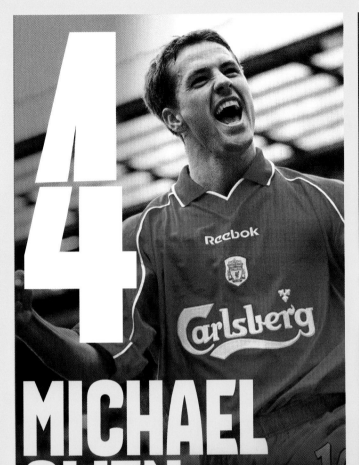

MICHAEL OWEN

150 PREM GOALS

Michael Owen scored his first goal on his debut for Liverpool at the age of 17, and then he just didn't stop! He finished his first full season in the Premier League as joint-top scorer – no wonder they nicknamed him Boy Wonder. In fact, little Mickey scored so many epic goals that he was awarded the Ballon D'Or in 2001 – the last Englishman to win it!

Best Prem goal? Megs one Newcastle defender by the halfway line, skins a second, sprints into the box and dinks the keeper to seal a hat-trick!

WOAH BOY!

Horseracing has been Michael's main passion since he retired from footy – he now has more than 100 horses at his stables in Chester!

3

WAYNE ROONEY

194 PREM GOALS

A raw talent who perfected his skills on the streets of Liverpool, Rooney combines power, pace and a footballing brain that would get the better of Albert Einstein! Who can forget the way he announced himself to the world – scoring an injury-time blaster from outside the box to help his boyhood club Everton beat Arsenal when he was just 16!

Best Prem goal? An overhead kick that flew past Joe Hart during a well tense Manchester derby – no-one had ever seen anything like it!

THREE AND IN!

Wazza's been awarded Match Of The Day's Goal Of The Season an epic three times!

▶▶▶ TURN OVER NOW!

2

THIERRY HENRY

175 PREM GOALS

Not so much a scorer of goals, more a creator of football art. Chipping keepers, burying pinpoint free-kicks, firing off spin volleys and back heels – you name it, Henry scored it! All his Prem strikes came for Arsenal, a club he left as all-time top scorer in 2007! Along the way he won two Premier League titles, three FA Cups, two PFA Player Of The Year awards and four Golden Boots – he really was the man!

Best Prem goal? Has his back to goal and a Man. United player breathing down his neck – but Henry flicks up the ball, spins and lobs the keeper. Scenes!

0.68

STAT'S AMAZING!

That's the number of goals that the fab Frenchman averaged per game during his eight seasons in English football!

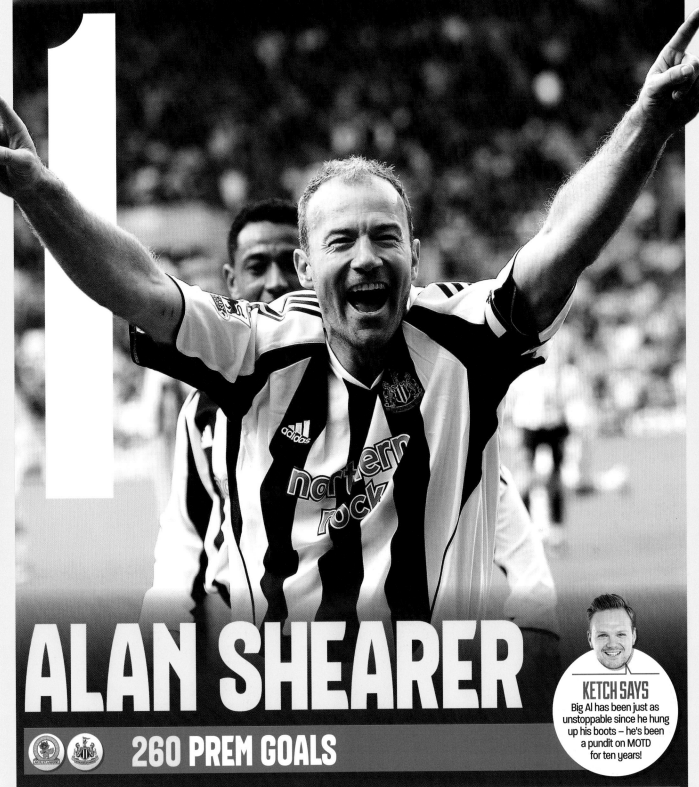

1

ALAN SHEARER

KETCH SAYS
Big Al has been just as unstoppable since he hung up his boots – he's been a pundit on MOTD for ten years!

260 PREM GOALS

The MOTD pundit is the only player in Prem history to go past the 200-goal mark – although he's likely to be joined by Wayne Rooney some time soon! Shearer smashed Newcastle's all-time goal record during his final ever season, and his last strike for The Toon came when it mattered most – on enemy territory during the Tyne-Wear Derby against Sunderland. Howay the lad!

Best Prem goal? A stupendous 25-yard volley at the Gallowgate End against Everton – it's possibly the hardest shot ever hit in Prem history!

2032

GET A MOVE ON!

Marcus Rashford will have to score 16 goals every season until 2032 if he wants to beat Alan Shearer's Prem record!

LIGUE 1

PSG
LIGUE 1 CHAMPIONS

2015-16

BARCELONA
LA LIGA CHAMPIONS

LEAGUE WINNERS

LEICESTER
PREMIER LEAGUE CHAMPIONS

CELTIC
SCOTTISH PREM CHAMPIONS

Ladbrokes PREMIERSHIP
15/16 WINNERS
CELTIC FOOTBALL CLUB

BAYERN MUNICH
BUNDESLIGA CHAMPIONS

JUVENTUS
SERIE A CHAMPIONS

LUIS SUAREZ
BARCELONA / 9

THIS IS THE SENSATIONAL STORY OF
EURO 2016

24 TEAMS · 51 MATCHES · 108 GOALS

FEATURING... 11 Viking warriors, 3 lousy lions, 1 Swansea reject, 1 giant moth, 1 ridiculous penalty shootout & much, much more...

THE GROUP STAGE

The battle of Britain, random headwear and loose-hips Ledley!

ALLEZ LES BLEUS!

France's Dimitri Payet scores a spectacular last-minute winner as the hosts kick-off the tournament with a 2-1 victory over Romania. The French remain unbeaten in the group stage and Payet pulls all the strings!

ENGLAND EDGE THE BATTLE OF BRITAIN...

The most talked-about game of the group stage is England's mouth-watering clash with Wales. The Three Lions snatch a 2-1 win thanks to Daniel Sturridge's dramatic injury-time goal – but it is to be England's ONLY win of the tournament. Sad face!

CHEERIO, ZLATAN!

It's a bad time to be Swedish. Not only do they fail to win a game in Group E – but star striker Zlatan Ibrahimovic then retires from international football!

...BUT WALES HAVE THE LAST LAUGH!

Despite that defeat, Wales go on to top the group thanks to a 3-0 win over Russia in the final game. Gareth Bale and Aaron Ramsey star, but it's the bearded boogie man Joe Ledley who captures the headlines – his celebration shuffle is a thing of beauty!

OI! WHAT ARE YOU WEARING, OLD-TIMER?

For some reason, Hungary's 40-year-old keeper Gabor Kiraly thinks it's okay to play in tracky bottoms!

THIS IS FOOTBALL, SIR – NOT A HAT CONVENTION!

A big-up to Croatia's Vedran Corluka for his splendid choice of in-game headwear!

THROUGH ➔ FRANCE, SWITZERLAND, WALES, ENGLAND, SLOVAKIA, GERMANY, POLAND, NORTHERN IRELAND, CROATIA, SPAIN, ITALY, BELGIUM, REPUBLIC OF IRELAND, HUNGARY, ICELAND, PORTUGAL

OUT ➔ ALBANIA, ROMANIA, RUSSIA, UKRAINE, TURKEY, CZECH REPUBLIC, SWEDEN, AUSTRIA

ROUND OF 16

Disaster for England, a clap-tastic Icelandic party and pain for Spain!

WELL, THAT WASN'T SUPPOSED TO HAPPEN!

It's utter humiliation for England as they slump to their most embarrassing defeat since losing to the USA in 1950. Iceland's stunning 2-1 victory spells the end for Roy Hodgson who quits as England boss and it also introduces the world to the incredible Icelandic Viking clap. Scenes!

ENGLAND AT EURO 2016
PLAYED 4   WINS 1   SCORED 4   CONCEDED 4
PEOPLE WHO THINK HARRY KANE SHOULD TAKE CORNERS 1 (ROY)

NO LUCK FOR THE IRISH!

The Irish are out! The Republic are done for by Antoine Griezmann, who scores twice for France in their 2-1 triumph, and Northern Ireland lose the second battle of Britain to Chris Coleman's in-form Wales!

HAZARD WARNING FOR EUROPE!

Two teams who are hitting form at the right time are Germany and Belgium. The Germans crush Slovakia 3-0 while Eden Hazard turns on the style to fire the impressive Belgians to a 4-0 win over Hungary!

ADIOS, SPANISH DUDES!

England aren't the only high-profile exiters at this stage though, as reigning champions Spain also crash out, losing 2-0 to an organised and tactically superior Italy!

XHERDAN THE HERO, XHAKA THE ZERO!

Stoke winger Xherdan Shaqiri scores the goal of the tournament – an acrobatic volley – but it isn't enough as the Swiss lose on penalties to Poland. It's actually another Premier League man, Arsenal's Granit Xhaka, who misses the crucial spot-kick!

THROUGH ➜ POLAND, PORTUGAL, WALES, BELGIUM, GERMANY, ITALY, FRANCE, ICELAND

OUT ➜ SWITZERLAND, CROATIA, NORTHERN IRELAND, HUNGARY, SLOVAKIA, SPAIN, REPUBLIC OF IRELAND, ENGLAND

THE QUARTER-FINALS

The end of the Vikings, the worst penalty ever and the Welsh Cruyff!

POLES AXED!

Another penalty shootout for Poland – but this time it's not a happy ending as they lose to Portugal after playing out a 1-1 draw!

FASTEST GOAL!

Robert Lewandowski's goal against Portugal – his first and only of the Euros – will be the fastest goal of the tournament, coming after 1 minute and 40 seconds!

AND YOU THOUGHT THE ENGLISH WERE BAD AT PENS!

Another shootout is needed to separate Euro heavyweights Italy and Germany – but this isn't to be any old shootout! A total of SEVEN penalties are missed, with West Ham forward Simone Zaza producing possibly the worst penalty of all time!

KANU BELIEVE IT'S NOT CRUYFF?

The Welsh fairytale continues with a 3-1 win over Belgium. The magical moment comes on 55 minutes when Hal Robson-Kanu does a stunning Cruyff Turn, sending three defenders the wrong way, before scoring Wales' second!

FRANCE TOO HOT FOR THE ICE MEN!

England's conquerors and tournament giant-killers Iceland finally meet their match. The loveable Vikings lose 5-2 to hosts and Euro 2016 favourites France. But what a tournament for the Ice Men! Altogether now... *clap* HUH, *clap* HUH, *clap* HUH, *clap* HUH! *clap* HUH! *clap* HUH!

THROUGH ➜ PORTUGAL, WALES, GERMANY, FRANCE

OUT ➜ POLAND, BELGIUM, ITALY, ICELAND

THE SEMI-FINALS

A meeting of Madrid megastars, heartbreak for Wales and Griezmann on flames!

RONALDO 1-0 BALE! PORTUGAL 2-0 WALES!

All eyes are on Cristiano Ronaldo and Gareth Bale as the Real Madrid team-mates clash for a place in the final. Wales, in their first tournament since 1958, are undone by two quick second-half Portuguese goals from Nani and Ronaldo. It's heartbreak for Wales, but Portugal are into the final for the first time since Euro 2004!

Incredibly, this is Portugal's FIRST win at Euro 2016 in normal time!

Did you know?

Cristiano Ronaldo becomes the first player to play in three Euro semi-finals (2004, 2012, 2016) and his goal equals Michel Platini's record of nine goals in Euro history!

ANTOINE IS THE MANN!

In the other semi-final, France's golden boy Antoine Griezmann takes centre stage with two goals in France's 2-0 win over Germany – and pretty much guarantees himself the golden boot!

Germany have now lost FOUR of their last six semi-finals at major tournaments!

Did you know?

This is France's first victory over Germany in a major tournament since the 1958 World Cup!

THROUGH ➜ PORTUGAL, FRANCE

OUT ➜ WALES, GERMANY

THE FINAL

Heartbreak for C-Ron, an unlikely hero and a big, fat hairy moth!

OH MY... PORTUGAL ARE CHAMPIONS OF EUROPE!

Thirty days after the first ball of Euro 2016 was kicked, we reach the final. Hosts France take on surprise team Portugal and, against all odds, it is the Portuguese who claim the unlikeliest of victories. Swansea reject Eder climbs off the substitutes' bench to score the winner, a 20-yard screamer, just 11 minutes from the end of extra-time. Amazing!

A TRAGIC END FOR RONALDO!

Just 25 minutes into the final, Portugal's go-to superstar Ronaldo is sensationally forced off with an injury – as you can imagine, C-Ron is devastated!

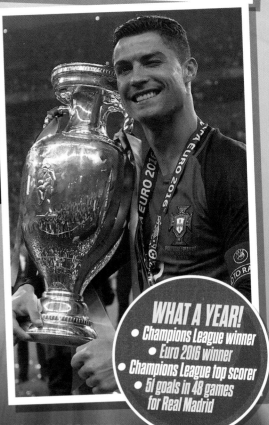

WHAT A YEAR!
- Champions League winner
- Euro 2016 winner
- Champions League top scorer
- 51 goals in 48 games for Real Madrid

CLATT'S THE WAY TO DO IT!
An Englishman DOES make the final after all – referee Mark Clattenburg is the man in the middle for this historic clash!

WHAT THE MOTH IS THAT ALL ABOUT?
As Ronaldo sits slumped on the turf, knowing his final is over, a cheeky French moth lands on the Real Madrid megastar's face and casually flaps away without a care in the world. What a ledge!

ALL HAIL RONALDO!
He may have been forced off through injury in the final, but for many experts Ronaldo was the star of the tournament and he's now finally done something Lionel Messi hasn't – won a major international tournament!

EURO 2016 AT A GLANCE

WINNER
PORTUGAL

PLAYER OF THE TOURNAMENT & TOP SCORER
ANTOINE GRIEZMANN
France, 6 goals

YOUNG PLAYER OF THE TOURNAMENT
RENATO SANCHES
Portugal

TEAM OF THE TOURNAMENT
FORMATION: 4-3-3

HUGO LLORIS
FRANCE

JOSHUA KIMMICH
GERMANY

PEPE
PORTUGAL

LEONARDO BONUCCI
ITALY

RAPHAEL GUERREIRO
PORTUGAL

AARON RAMSEY
WALES

TONI KROOS
GERMANY

DIMITRI PAYET
FRANCE

GARETH BALE
WALES

ANTOINE GRIEZMANN
FRANCE

CRISTIANO RONALDO
PORTUGAL

TOURNAMENT STATS!

MOST ASSISTS
Aaron Ramsey, Wales &
Eden Hazard, Belgium, 4

MOST CLEAN SHEETS
Manuel Neuer, Germany
& Rui Patricio, Portugal, 4

MOST GOALS SCORED
France, 13

FEWEST GOALS SCORED
Ukraine, 0

BIGGEST WIN
Belgium 4-0 Hungary

HIGHEST ATTENDANCE
France vs Iceland,
76,833

LOWEST ATTENDANCE
Russia vs Wales, 28,840

MESSI QUIZ!

What can you tell us about the Barcelona and Argentina hero?

Q1 HOW OLD IS LEO?
29, 30 or 32?

Q2 IN WHICH ARGENTINIAN CITY WAS HE BORN?
Buenos Aires or Rosario?

ANSWER

Q3 WHICH TEAM DID HE JOIN BARCELONA FROM?
Newell's Old Boys or River Plate?

ANSWER

Q4 IS HE RIGHT OR LEFT-FOOTED?

Q5 WORDSEARCH!
Find the five words related to little Leo to gain a point!

I	S	S	E	M	M	A	E	T
B	A	L	L	E	R	N	N	E
I	B	U	G	Y	F	I	X	K
B	Z	X	U	I	T	T	B	K
C	D	P	E	D	X	N	Q	E
Z	F	W	O	U	J	E	C	R
E	B	J	E	J	U	G	F	S
A	N	O	L	E	C	R	A	B
B	O	I	E	W	C	A	H	Z

TEAMMESSI
BALLER
BARCELONA
ARGENTINA
TEKKERS

Q6 TRUE OR FALSE? Leo's first ever Barcelona contract was written on a napkin!

ANSWER

Q7+8 BACK OF THE NET!
Which two clubs has Messi never scored against?

ANSWER   ANSWER

Q9 GOLD STANDARD!
Which trophy has Messi won the most?

CHAMPIONS LEAGUE

LA LIGA

ANSWER

BALLON D'OR

FIFA CLUB WORLD CUP

Q10 WELL GROUNDED!
Where does Messi play his home games for Barca?

ANSWER

YOUR SCORE

/10

ANSWERS ON p92!

THE FANTA

WHERE ARE THEY

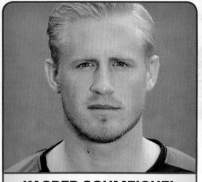

KASPER SCHMEICHEL
AGE IN 2046: 59

Returned to his native Denmark after helping Leicester to Champions League glory in 2019. The 59-year-old ex-Foxes No.1 now runs a zoo in the Danish capital Copenhagen and is the reigning Hungry Hippos world champion!

DANNY SIMPSON
AGE IN 2046: 59

Danny quit the UK for a life of showbiz in 2022. His weekly magic show – Don't Call Me Bart – at Caesar's Palace, in Las Vegas, USA, is now officially the most successful magic show in American history, smashing all box-office records!

ROBERT HUTH
AGE IN 2046: 61

The 61-year-old ex-Leicester centre-back is now the manager of Indian Super League club Mumbai City, owner of a luxury health spa for stressed-out chimpanzees and currently dating ex-British Prime Minister Theresa May!

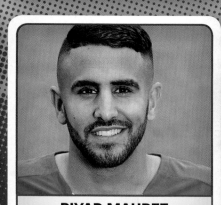

DANNY DRINKWATER
AGE IN 2046: 56

Quit football in 2021 to concentrate on his dream of becoming Lancashire's No.1 butcher. He now owns a chain of shops in Bury and Oldham and the Rochdale Gazette recently praised Drinkwater's gloriously juicy sausages!

MARC ALBRIGHTON
AGE IN 2046: 56

Currently travelling to Mars as part of NASA's latest attempt to enable humankind to live on the red planet. He is onboard space shuttle Orion with TV presenter Eamon Holmes, ex-Newcastle defender Titus Bramble and Coronation Street's Steve McDonald!

RIYAD MAHREZ
AGE IN 2046: 55

Actor. Currently playing Tybalt to rave reviews in Shakespeare's Romeo & Juliet at the Novello Theatre in London. Poised to play the role of Han Solo's cousin in Star Wars XVIII: Revenge Attack Of The Phantom Jedi Clones – out this summer!

STIC FOXES!
NOW?

We've fast-forwarded to the year 2046 – three decades on from Leicester's incredible title win to see what their heroes of 2016 are getting up to in their post-footy lives...

THE CLASS OR 2016 30 YEARS ON!

WES MORGAN
AGE IN 2046: 62

Now into his fifth year as host of Radio Leicester's Drivetime slot. Wes is the reigning East Midlands Radio Presenter Of The Year. He's also chairman of the Peppa Pig Appreciation Society and inventor of the invisible teabag!

CHRISTIAN FUCHS
AGE IN 2046: 60

After spells managing Rapid Vienna, Inter Milan, Porto, Galatasaray, Auxerre, Cameroon, Benin, Al-Hilal, 1860 Munich, Fortuna Dusseldorf, Greece, Oman, Syria, Chievo, Parma and AC Milan, Christian is now assistant manager of Lidl in Halifax!

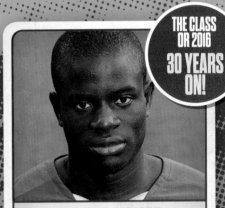

N'GOLO KANTE
AGE IN 2046: 55

Host of smash-hit TV show If Anyone Can, Kante Can. The Frenchman, dressed in his familiar wizard costume and polka-dot cape, attempts a new, seemingly impossible challenge every week. Also manager of non-league Dulwich Hamlet!

SHINJI OKAZAKI
AGE IN 2046: 60

Okazaki hit the headlines in the summer of 2024 when a national newspaper revealed that he is a distant cousin of Pokemon fave Pikachu. Now retired to the Tokyo suburbs, Shinji hosts regular Pokemon parties for besotted fans!

JAMIE VARDY
AGE IN 2046: 59

Following his sensational decision to quit football in January 2017, just eight months after winning the Premier League, Jamie lives in an ice-cream van parked outside Buckingham Palace, refusing to speak to anyone but his pet raccoon Dave!

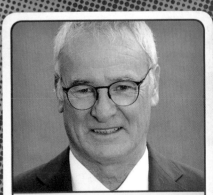

CLAUDIO RANIERI
AGE IN 2046: 94

Now in his 32nd season as boss of Leicester. Sir Claudio is the most successful manager in English football history after guiding The Foxes to 19 Premier League titles, 15 FA Cup wins and 12 Champions League successes. The club are also the current Global Super League champs!

GUESS WHO?

ANSWERS ON p92!

Name the missing players — get a point for each one you get right!

3 LEICESTER
2015-16
Premier League title-winning team

Schmeichel

Simpson   Morgan   Huth   Fuchs

.... Kante

Mahrez   Albrighton

Was it...   Vardy   Okazaki

A Drinkwater ☐   B King ☐   C Inler ☐

4 ENGLAND
2016
Friendly v Germany, March

Butland

.... Cahill   Smalling   Rose

Henderson   Dier

Welbeck   Alli   Lallana

Was it...   Kane

A Walker ☐   B Milner ☐   C Clyne ☐

1 REAL MADRID
2015-16
Champions League final

Navas

Carvajal   Ramos   Pepe   Marcelo

Kroos   ....   Modric

Bale   Ronaldo

Was it...   Benzema

A Isco ☐   B Casemiro ☐   C James Rodriguez ☐

5 MAN. UNITED
2015-16
FA Cup final

De Gea

Valencia   Smalling   Blind   Rojo

Carrick   Rooney

Mata   ....   Martial

Was it...   Rashford

A Fellaini ☐   B Lingard ☐   C Young ☐

2 PORTUGAL
2016
Euro 2016 final

Patricio

Soares   Pepe   Fonte   Guerreiro

W. Carvalho

Sanches   Silva   Joao Mario

Was it...   Ronaldo   ....

A Eder ☐   B Moutinho ☐   C Nani ☐

6 MAN. CITY
2015-16
Capital One Cup final

Caballero

Sagna   Kompany   Otamendi   Clichy

Fernando   Fernandinho

Toure

Was it...   Silva   Aguero   ....

A Bony ☐   B Sterling ☐   C Iheanacho ☐

SANCHEZ
ARSENAL / 7

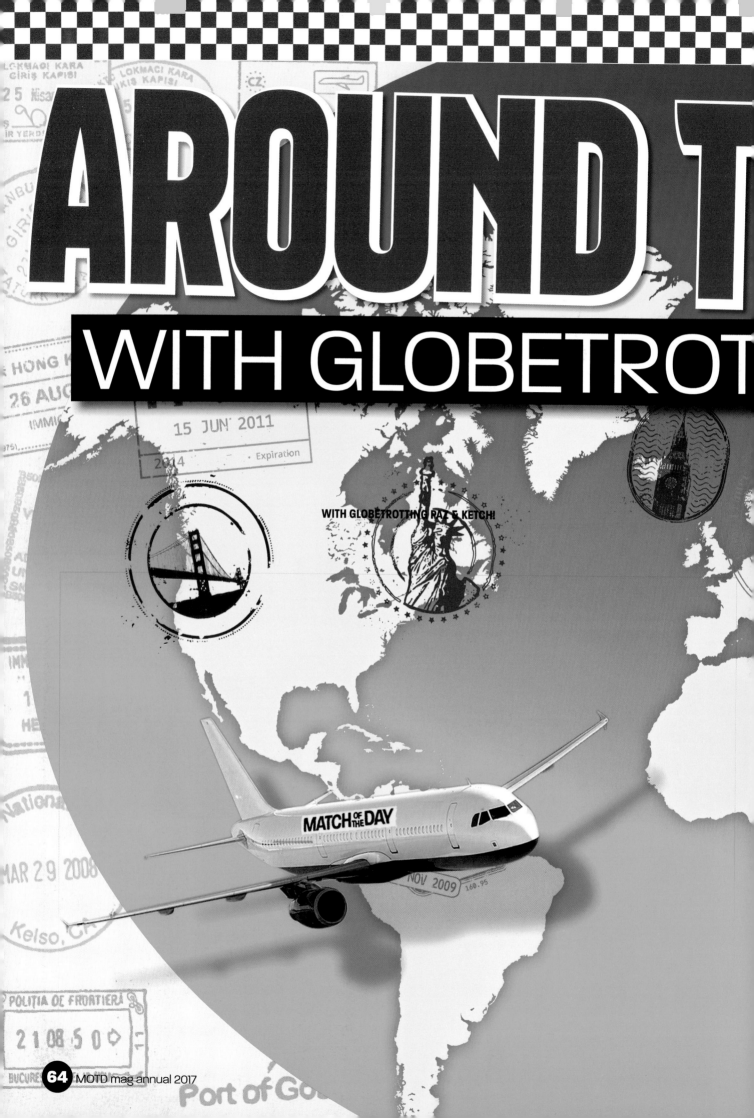

AROUND T
WITH GLOBETROT

WITH GLOBETROTTING RAZ & KETCH!

MATCH OF THE DAY

AFRICA

No. of countries: 54
Area: 30,370,000 km²
Total population: 1.1 billion
Biggest city: Lagos, Nigeria
(population 16.1 million)

BEST PLAYER NOW
PIERRE-EMERICK AUBAMEYANG
GABON & BORUSSIA DORTMUND
Speedy frontman who was African Player Of The Year last season after hitting 39 goals in just 46 games!

BEST PLAYER EVER
SAMUEL ETO'O
CAMEROON
Striker who scored 129 goals in 201 games for Barcelona between 2004 and 2009, helping the club to lift three La Liga titles and two Champions League trophies!

★★★ MOST SUCCESSFUL CLUB
Al Ahly, Egypt
8 x African champions

PYRAMIDS OF GIZA ★

MOST SUCCESSFUL NATION
Egypt 7 x African champions

FOOTBALL IN AFRICA
FIFA confederation
Confederation Of African Football (CAF)
CAF HQ Egypt Formed 1957
Member countries 56

Africa's most dangerous animal is not the lion, bear or crocodile – it's the hippo! He may look big and fat but this lumbering beast is believed to kill more people per year than any other mammal!

SERENGETI NATIONAL PARK ★

★ **MOUNT KILIMANJARO**

VICTORIA FALLS ★

BIGGEST STADIUM
FNB Stadium Johannesburg
South Africa **94,736**

TABLE MOUNTAIN ★

★ **FAMOUS ATTRACTIONS**

ASIA

FOOTBALL IN ASIA
FIFA confederation
Asian Football Confederation (AFC)
AFC HQ Malaysia Formed: 1954
Member countries: 47

BEST PLAYER NOW
SHINJI OKAZAKI
JAPAN & LEICESTER
Hardworking striker who helped fire The Foxes to an incredible Premier League title success in 2015-16!

No. of countries: 48
Area: 44,579,000 km²
Total population: 4.1 billion
Biggest city: Shanghai, China
(population 24.3 million)

BEST PLAYER EVER
CHA BUM-KUN
SOUTH KOREA
Explosive striker from the 1970s and '80s who starred in the Bundesliga and for his country, for whom he is the all-time record scorer!

BIGGEST STADIUM
Rungrado May Day Stadium
Pyongyang, North Korea
150,000

We've got to big up Iranian legend Ali Daei. Between 1993 and his retirement in 2006 he scored 109 goals in 150 games making him the world's all-time international record goalscorer!

★ **PETRA**

MOUNT EVEREST ★

GREAT WALL OF CHINA

TAJ MAHAL ★

ANGKOR WAT ★

MOST SUCCESSFUL NATION
Japan 4 x Asian champions

MOST SUCCESSFUL CLUB
Pohang Steelers
South Korea
3 x Asian champions

EUROPE

FOOTBALL IN EUROPE

FIFA confederation
Union Of European Football
Associations (UEFA)

UEFA HQ Switzerland Formed 1954
Member countries 55

No. of countries: 50
Area: 10,180,000 km^2
Total population: 742 million
Biggest city: Istanbul, Turkey (population 14.2 million)

MOST SUCCESSFUL CLUB
Real Madrid, Spain
11 x European champions

BIG BEN

MOST SUCCESSFUL NATION
Germany
4 x World Cup winners

EIFFEL
TOWER

LEANING TOWER
OF PISA

SAGRADA
FAMILIA

COLOSSEUM

BIGGEST STADIUM
Nou Camp
Barcelona, Spain
99,354

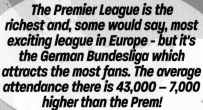

The Premier League is the richest and, some would say, most exciting league in Europe - but it's the German Bundesliga which attracts the most fans. The average attendance there is 43,000 – 7,000 higher than the Prem!

BEST PLAYER NOW

CRISTIANO RONALDO PORTUGAL & REAL MADRID
A phenomenon who's scored 364 goals in 348 games for Real Madrid – and who, last season, won the Euros and his third Champions League!

BEST PLAYER EVER

ZINEDINE ZIDANE FRANCE
The most technically gifted European of all time, who just pips Johan Cruyff to this title, was a midfield genius for Juventus and Real Madrid between 1996 and 2006!

▶▶▶ **TURN OVER FOR MORE!**

NORTH AMERICA

No. of countries: 23
Area: 24,709,000 km²
Total population: 565 million
Biggest city: Mexico City, Mexico (population 8.9 million)

BIGGEST STADIUM
Aztec Stadium
Mexico City, Mexico
84,000

MOST SUCCESSFUL CLUB
Club America, Mexico
7 x CONCACAF champions

MOST SUCCESSFUL NATION
Mexico 10 x CONCACAF champions

> Mexico have bossed this region – but the rise of the MLS and growing popularity of soccer in America is helping Team USA build solid footy foundations!

YELLOWSTONE NATIONAL PARK
★

NIAGARA FALLS

GRAND CANYON
★

STATUE OF LIBERTY
★

CHICHEN ITZA

BEST PLAYER NOW
JAVIER HERNANDEZ
MEXICO & BAYER LEVERKUSEN
Goal-poaching specialist who hit 26 goals last season and was named in the Bundesliga Team Of The Year!

BEST PLAYER EVER
HUGO SANCHEZ MEXICO
Legendary striker, famed for his acrobatic overhead kicks, who bagged 208 goals in 283 games for Spanish giants Real Madrid between 1985 and 1992!

AUSTRALIA

Includes New Zealand & neighbouring Pacific Islands

No. of countries: 14
Area: 8,526,000 km²
Total population: 37 million
Biggest city: Sydney, Australia (population 4.9 million)

GREAT BARRIER REEF
★

BIGGEST STADIUM
ANZ Stadium Sydney, Australia
83,500

ULURU
★

> Strewth! In 2006, Australia quit the Oceania Football Confederation to join the Asian Confederation – The Socceroos think it gives them a better chance of qualifying for the World Cup!

SYDNEY OPERA HOUSE
★

BONDI BEACH

BEST PLAYER NOW
AARON MOOY
HUDDERSFIELD & AUSTRALIA
Midfielder who joined Man. City from Melbourne City in the summer, before being loaned out to The Terriers for 2016-17!

BEST PLAYER EVER
HARRY KEWELL
AUSTRALIA
Skilful left-winger who starred for Leeds between 1997 and 2003, being named Oceania Player Of The Year three times in five years!

MOST SUCCESSFUL NATION
Australia 4 x Oceania champions

MOST SUCCESSFUL CLUB
Auckland City, New Zealand
8 x Oceania champions

SOUTH AMERICA

FOOTBALL IN SOUTH AMERICA
FIFA confederation
South American Football
Confederation (CONMEBOL)
CAF HQ Paraguay Formed 1916
Member countries 10

★ ANGEL FALLS

★ THE AMAZON RAINFOREST

★ MACHU PICCHU

★ CHRIST THE REDEEMER

No. of countries: 12
Area: 17,840,000 km²
Total population: 386 million
Biggest city: Sao Paulo,
Brazil (population 11.9 million)

Brazil may be the most successful international team in the world – but when it comes to club football in South America, the Argentinians rule. Boca Juniors, Independiente and River Plate are the continent's top dogs!

BEST PLAYER NOW
LIONEL MESSI
ARGENTINA & BARCELONA
He's scored a mind-boggling 456 goals in 535 games for Barcelona, won FIVE Ballon D'Or trophies, four Champions League trophies and eight La Liga titles!

MOST SUCCESSFUL NATION
Brazil 5 x World Cup winners

BIGGEST STADIUM
Estadio Monumental
Lima. Peru **80,093**

MOST SUCCESSFUL CLUB
Boca Juniors, Argentina
6 x South American champions

BEST PLAYER EVER
LIONEL MESSI **ARGENTINA**
Pele and Diego Maradona fans may disagree, but the numbers, the stats and the breath-taking ability doesn't lie!

MAN.
CITY
21

DAVID
SILVA

THE MOTD FOOTY DICTIONARY!

Football is a universal language, so MOTD mag has invented some terms to help you speak it fluently!

THE MOTD DICTIONARY

4TH-ENAL

Number
To finish fourth, or in the position after bronze
● *"Gold, silver, bronze, 4th-enal"*
ORIGIN Arsenal's regular top-four finishes!

COSTA

Noun
Feeling or showing anger, displeasure or hostility
● *"Easy man – no need to get all Costa about it"*
ORIGIN Diego Costa's angry pitch tantrums!

HODGSON

Noun
The inability to do something successfully
● *"That's total Hodgson, mate"*
ORIGIN Roy Hodgson's disastrous period as England boss!

JOSE

Noun
A long, bitter feud
● *"They had a massive Jose over whose turn it was to empty the bin"*
ORIGIN Jose Mourinho's petty quarrels with refs, fans, owners, players and his own dog!

LEICESTER

Noun
An unlikely event that brings about great joy and happiness
● *"It's an absolute Leicester that they've managed to do that"*
● *"Come on mate, I can't produce Leicesters at the drop of a hat"*
ORIGIN The incredible chain of events that led to Leicester lifting the 2015-16 Prem title!

POGBA

Adjective
Costing a lot of money
● *"Wow, I bet those boots cost a Pogba or two"*
ORIGIN Named after the most expensive player in the world – Man. United megastar Paul Pogba!

PULIS

Noun
An object that won't sink
● *"There was a stinky Pulis floating in the water"*
ORIGIN Tony Pulis' canny knack of keeping clubs afloat in the Prem!

QUARESMA

Verb
To pass using the outside of the foot
● *"He Quaresmaed it around the wall and into the net"*
● *"Quick, hit me with a Quaresma"*
ORIGIN Named after Portugal and Besiktas midfield man Ricardo Quaresma – who hits 98.7% of his passes with the outside of his boot!

RASHFORD

Noun
Something, or someone, that's extremely young
● *"Go easy on them, they're still just Rashfords"*
● *"That little Rashford is always crying"*
ORIGIN Marcus Rashford who scored his first senior goal shortly after graduating from nursery school!

RONALDO

Adjective
In good health due to frequent exercise and dedication
● *"He was well Ronaldo, he never stopped all game"*
ORIGIN Megastar Cristiano Ronaldo's dedication to his personal fitness!

SHAQIRI

Noun
A perfectly executed overhead kick
● *"Wow, did you see that Shaqiri hit the back of the net?"*
ORIGIN Xherdan Shaqiri's Euro 2016 belter!

WENGER

Noun
A person who hates spending money
● *"Oh, he's a right Wenger"*
ORIGIN Arsene Wenger's refusal to spend his mega transfer kitty!

WILSHERE

Noun
The ankle joint
● *"I can't play, I've injured my Wilshere... again"*
ORIGIN Wilshere's injury problems!

VARDY

Noun
An impossible record
● *"You'll never get the Vardy"*
● *"He's only gone and broke the Vardy"*
ORIGIN Jamie Vardy's Prem record of scoring in 11 games in a row!

MY *DREAM TEAM* FC!

Your chance to build a superclub — you pick the name, the players, the kit. Everything!

CLUB FACT FILE!

CLUB NAME

CLUB NICKNAME

STADIUM NAME

STADIUM CAPACITY

MANAGER   YOUR NAME

YOUR AGE

CLUB COLOURS

STICK YOUR PHOTO HERE

CLUB BADGE!

Design your club's badge!

KITS!

Design your club's HOME kit!

Design your club's AWAY kit!

Oh, badge! I thought you said badger!

Which superstars will make your team?

MY STARTING 11!

PLAYER PHOTO IN HERE!

KEEPER

PLAYER PHOTO IN HERE!

PLAYER PHOTO IN HERE!

PLAYER PHOTO IN HERE!

PLAYER PHOTO IN HERE!

RIGHT-BACK   **CENTRE-BACK**   **CENTRE-BACK**   **LEFT-BACK**

PLAYER PHOTO IN HERE!

PLAYER PHOTO IN HERE!

MIDFIELDER   **MIDFIELDER**

PLAYER PHOTO IN HERE!

PLAYER PHOTO IN HERE!

PLAYER PHOTO IN HERE!

FORWARD   **FORWARD**   **FORWARD**

PLAYER PHOTO IN HERE!

STRIKER

CAPTAIN   **VICE-CAPTAIN**   **PENALTY TAKER**

CLUB SCARF!

Design your club's scarf!

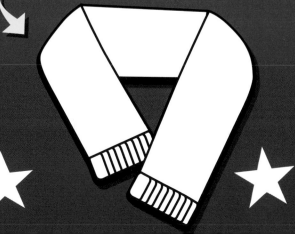

PLAYING STYLE!

ATTACKING ☐   DEFENSIVE ☐

PASSING ☐   COUNTER ☐

DIRECT ☐   PATIENT ☐

LONG-BALL ☐   HIGH TEMPO ☐

ANTOINE GRIEZMANN
ATLETICO MADRID / 7

100%
football

100%
random!

▶▶▶ TURN OVER NOW!

10 FOOTBALLERS WHO LIKE TO HANG OUT WITH ANIMALS

WAYNE ROONEY AND A TIGER

AARON RAMSEY AND A LEMUR

LUKAS PODOLSKI, MESUT OZIL AND A LION

FRANCK RIBERY AND A BABY LION

ARJEN ROBBEN, BASTIAN SCHWEINSTEIGER, MANUEL NEUER AND A CAMEL

MAMADOU SAKHO AND A KOALA

PATRICE EVRA AND A SNOW LEOPARD

6 fuzzy footballers with whiskerlicious beards

JOE LEDLEY
CRYSTAL PALACE

MICHAEL BOSTWICK
PETERBOROUGH

MARCO SAILER
FSV WACKER

RAUL MEIRELES
FENERBAHCE

MARC CROSAS
TENERIFE

NAT BORCHERS
PORTLAND TIMBERS

4 utterly random photos of John Terry doing stuff in China

▶▶▶ TURN OVER FOR MORE!

3 photos of ex-Spain boss Vicente Del Bosque wondering if he left the oven on

1 incredible photo of a footballer getting hit in the face by the ball

DAVID MENDES DA SILVA
SPARTA ROTTERDAM

5 MANAGERS AS YOU'VE NEVER SEEN THEM BEFORE

JOACHIM LOW

RONALD KOEMAN

ZINEDINE ZIDANE

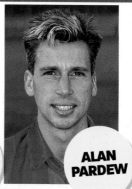

ALAN PARDEW

MARK HUGHES

7 teams who totally messed up their team photo

REAL VALLADOLID 2001
Why'd you get a comedy cartoon castle involved?

SANTOS 2010
Why'd you invite those things along and get the photo taken from a crane?

MAN. UNITED 2003
Why'd you not switch your phones off?

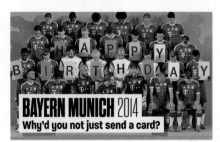
BAYERN MUNICH 2014
Why'd you not just send a card?

YOKOHAMA F. MARINOS 2004
Why'd you sign a duck and 11 kids?

GHANA WOMEN U-20 2014
Why'd you start walking on your knees?

CAMEROON WOMEN 2015
Why'd you not line up like normal teams?

3 HAIRCUTS THAT SHOULD BE PUT IN A MUSEUM AND REMEMBERED FOREVER

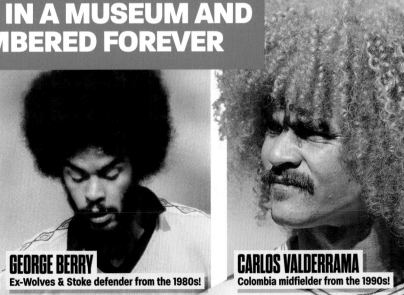

PETER BORATA
Ex-Chelsea keeper from the early 1980s!

GEORGE BERRY
Ex-Wolves & Stoke defender from the 1980s!

CARLOS VALDERRAMA
Colombia midfielder from the 1990s!

▶▶▶ TURN OVER FOR MORE!

2 FOOTBALLERS WHO DON'T KNOW HOW TO HOLD A PEN

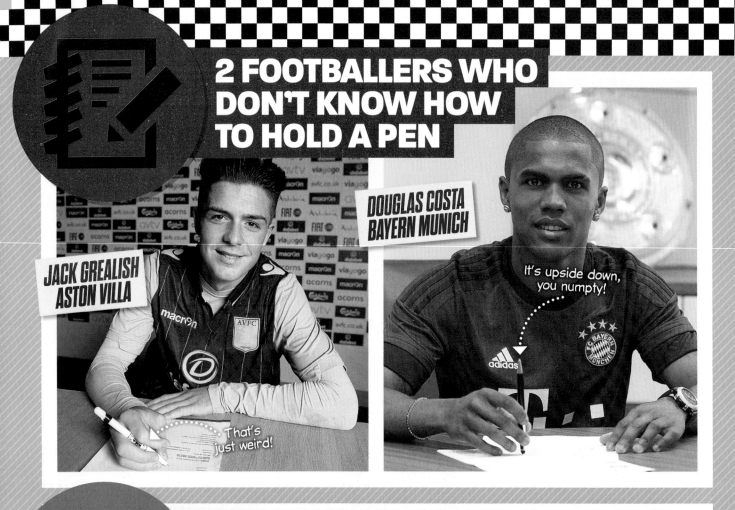

JACK GREALISH
ASTON VILLA

That's just weird!

DOUGLAS COSTA
BAYERN MUNICH

It's upside down, you numpty!

4 CATS THAT LOOK LIKE JOSE MOURINHO

1

2

3

4

6 CLUB BADGES THAT NEED TO BE SEEN TO BE BELIEVED

COBRESAL

BANGKOK GLASS FOOTBALL CLUB

AVENIR BEGGEN

LINCOLN CITY FC

GOMBAK UNITED FOOTBALL CLUB

DETROIT CITY FC

3 OF THE MOST INCREDIBLE MOUSTACHES IN FOOTBALL HISTORY

FRANS STRUIS
DUTCH PLAYER FROM THE 1970s

ARTUR JORGE
EX-PORTUGUESE PLAYER & MANAGER

ABE VAN DEN BAN
DUTCH PLAYER FROM THE 1970s & '80s

▶▶▶ TURN OVER FOR MORE!

20 FOOTY CLUBS THAT HAVE GOT BONKERS NAMES

DEPORTIVO MORON
ARGENTINA

MIDDELFART
DENMARK

KING FAISAL BABES
GHANA

EBUSUA DWARFS
GHANA

CHICKEN INN FC
ZIMBABWE

DANDY TOWN HORNETS
BERMUDA

JOE PUBLIC FC
TRINIDAD & TOBAGO

INSURANCE MANAGEMENT BEARS FC
TRINIDAD & TOBAGO

BIG PLAYERS FC
ST LUCIA

HUMBLE LIONS
JAMAICA

GOOD LUCK FC
MARTINIQUE

BOTSWANA MEAT COMMISSION FC
BOTSWANA

BOBO SPORT
BURKINA FASO

ETHIOPIAN COFFEE FC
ETHIOPIA

INVINCIBLE ELEVEN
LIBERIA

MIGHTY BLUE ANGELS FC
LIBERIA

BIG BULLETS FC
MALAWI

YOUNG BUFFALOES FC
SWAZILAND

RHINO RANGERS FC
TANZANIA

TRIANGLE UNITED FC
ZIMBABWE

3 photos of Arsene Wenger doing that weird squatting thing he does

4 FOOTBALL HEROES LARKING ABOUT WITH A CUP ON THEIR HEAD

7 CLASSIC PHOTOS OF PEP GUARDIOLA GETTING SOAKED

FIRMINO

LIVERPOOL 11

THE ULTIMATE A-Z OF FOOTBALL QUIZ!

▶▶▶ TURN OVER FOR THE QUESTIONS!

A

ANSWER

A IS FOR... Henrikh Mkhitaryan secured a dream move to Man. United this year – but which country does he play for?

B

ANSWER

IS FOR... Which Championship club does this badge belong to? Clue – they play in London!

C

ANSWER

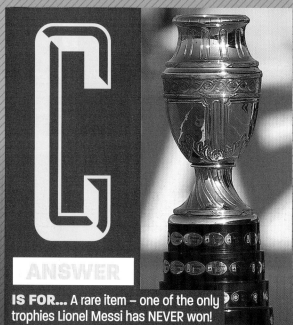

IS FOR... A rare item – one of the only trophies Lionel Messi has NEVER won!

D

ANSWER

IS FOR... Real Madrid's Brazilian right-back – name him!

E

IS FOR... A legendary Dutch midfielder who was nicknamed The Pitbull – but what's his first name?

ANSWER

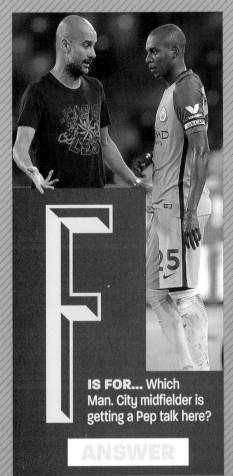

F

IS FOR... Which Man. City midfielder is getting a Pep talk here?

ANSWER

G

ANSWER

IS FOR... This man's name was the most sung in football last season – can you remember his surname!

H

IS FOR... You can get 25,586 Tigers in here – whose ground is it?

ANSWER

IS FOR... An Argentinian goal-getter who has played most of his career in Italy!

I

ANSWER

J

IS FOR... Romelu Lukaku's younger bro made one appearance alongside him at this year's Euros – what's Little Lukaku's first name?

ANSWER

K

IS FOR... This guy (in the middle) used to play for Liverpool and also managed England, Newcastle & Man. City!

ANSWER

L

IS FOR... Can you name the Midlands city where MOTD presenter Gary Lineker was born?

ANSWER

▶▶▶ **TURN OVER FOR M-Z!**

M

IS FOR... A rare boot brand that was founded in Japan 110 years ago. Name it!

N

IS FOR... These three have 319 international caps between them – in which US city do they now play?

O

IS FOR... This Norwegian whizzkid was signed by Real Madrid for £3.4m – but what's his surname?

P

IS FOR... A controlled, deliberate deflection by a keeper is known as a _ _ _ _ _ !

Q

IS FOR... A club nicknamed The Hoops and also the place where Raheem Sterling started his career!

R

IS FOR... This Swede managed England at three major tournaments!

S

IS FOR... Name the very big country hosting the World Cup in 2018!

T
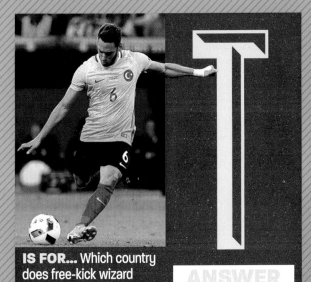

IS FOR... Which country does free-kick wizard Hakan Calhanoglu play for?

ANSWER

U

IS FOR... A 30-year-old striker who has played for Brighton and Leicester!

ANSWER

V
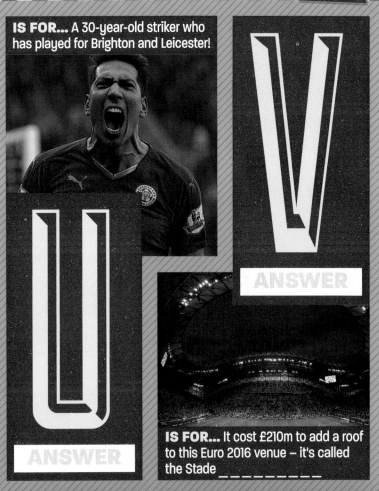

ANSWER

IS FOR... It cost £210m to add a roof to this Euro 2016 venue – it's called the Stade _ _ _ _ _ _ _ _ _

W

IS FOR... Which team does FIFA's strongest man, Adebayo 'The Beast' Akinfenwa, play for?

ANSWER

X

IS FOR... These brothers played against each other in a Euro 2016 group game – what's their surname?

ANSWER

ANSWER

Y Z

IS FOR... He's one of the most-wanted wingers in Europe – but can you spell Andriy's surname? Y _ RM _ LE _ K _

ANSWER

IS FOR... Which Russian top-flight club does this cool badge belong to?

▶▶▶ **ALL ANSWERS REVEALED ON p92!**

EDEN HAZARD

CHELSEA

10

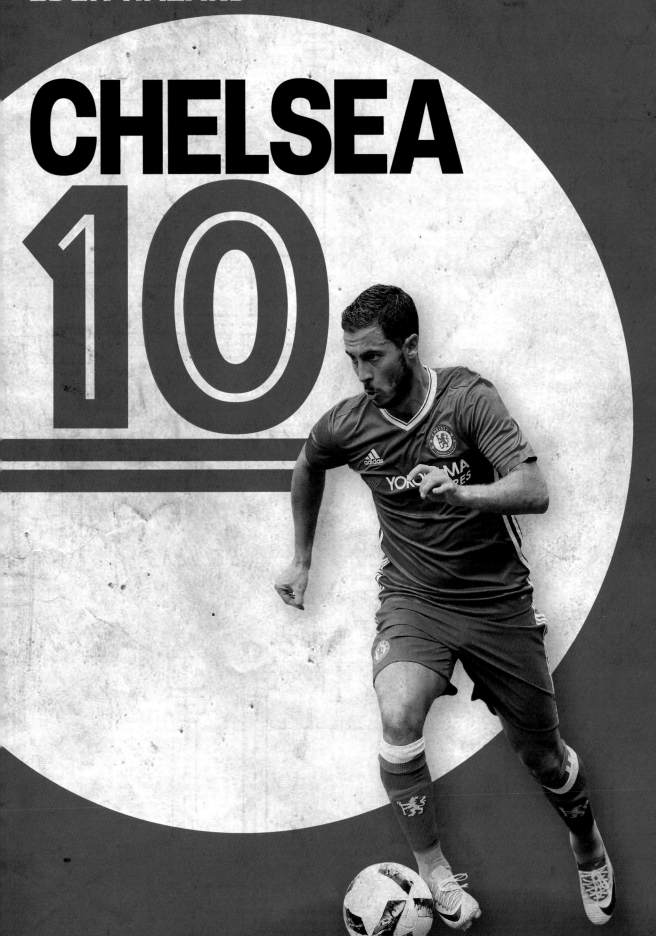

ANSWERS!

QUIZ 1 FROM PAGE 15
RONALDO QUIZ ANSWERS
1 31
2 Funchal
3 Sporting Lisbon
4 Right-footed
5 Answers below

L	T	G	C	O	B	J	G	R
A	I	P	J	S	X	O	E	Z
G	C	C	N	X	A	N	O	C
U	Z	X	K	L	N	D	T	O
T	X	H	S	I	L	C	E	H
R	M	Z	W	A	P	L	L	B
O	T	G	N	E	A	H	B	Q
P	M	O	S	E	S	I	V	R
G	R	Y	R	H	D	Z	N	Q

6 True
7+8 PSG & Benfica
9 Ballon D'Or
10 Bernabeu

MY SCORE [ANSWER] OUT OF 10

QUIZ 2 FROM PAGE 27
SPELLING TEST ANSWERS
1 Henrikh Mkhitaryan
2 Koke
3 Ilkay Gundogan
4 Daniel Carvajal
5 Robert Lewandowski
6 Alexis Sanchez
7 Sergio Busquets
8 Thiago Silva
9 Eden Hazard

MY SCORE [ANSWER] OUT OF 9

● Aubameyang was the 2015 African Player Of The Year!

● C-Ron won his first ever international trophy in 2016!

QUIZ 3 FROM PAGE 37
MATCH THE FACTS ANSWERS
1 C
2 F
3 B
4 E
5 A
6 D
7 H
8 G

MY SCORE [ANSWER] OUT OF 8

QUIZ 4 FROM PAGE 59
MESSI QUIZ ANSWERS
1 29
2 Rosario
3 Newell's Old Boys
4 Left-footed
5 Answers below

I	S	S	E	M	M	A	E	T
B	A	L	L	E	R	N	N	E
I	B	U	G	Y	F	I	X	K
B	Z	X	U	I	T	T	B	K
C	D	P	E	D	X	N	Q	E
Z	F	W	O	U	J	E	C	R
E	B	J	E	J	U	G	F	S
A	N	O	L	E	C	R	A	B
B	O	I	E	W	C	A	H	Z

6 True
7+8 Liverpool & Chelsea
9 La Liga
10 Nou Camp

MY SCORE [ANSWER] OUT OF 10

QUIZ 5 FROM PAGE 62
GUESS WHO ANSWERS
1 B, Casemiro
2 C, Nani
3 A, Drinkwater
4 C, Clyne
5 A, Fellaini
6 B, Sterling

MY SCORE [ANSWER] OUT OF 6

QUIZ 6 FROM PAGE 85
A-Z QUIZ ANSWERS

A Armenia	**B** Brentford
C Copa America	**D** Danilo
E Edgar	**F** Fernandinho
G Grigg	**H** Hull
I Icardi	**J** Jordan
K Kevin Keegan	**L** Leicester
M Mizuno	**N** New York City
O Odegaard	**P** Parry
Q QPR	**R** Russia
S Sven	**T** Turkey
U Ulloa	**V** Velodrome
W Wycombe	**X** Xhaka
Y Yarmolenko	**Z** Zenit St Petersburg

MY SCORE [ANSWER] OUT OF 26

MATCH OF THE DAY
MAGAZINE

Coutinho

Alli

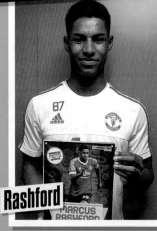
Rashford

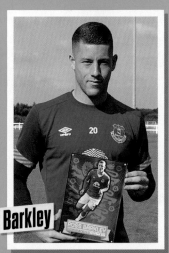
Barkley

THE BIGGEST SUPERSTARS EVERY WEEK!

Aguero

THE UK'S BEST-SELLING FOOTY MAG!

MATCH OF THE DAY

Write to us at
Match Of The Day magazine
Immediate Media, Vineyard
House, 44 Brook Green,
Hammersmith,
London, W6 7BT

Telephone 020 7150 5513
Email shout@motdmag.com
pazandketch@motdmag.com
www.motdmag.com

Match Of The Day editor	Ian Foster
Annual editor	Mark Parry
Art editor	Blue Buxton
Designer	Alastair Parr
News editor	Matthew Ketchell
Writer	Lee Stobbs
Group picture editor	Natasha Thompson
Picture editor	Jason Timson

Production editor	Neil Queen-Jones
Dep. production editor	Joe Shackley
Publishing consultant	Jaynie Bye
Editorial director	Corinna Shaffer
Annual images	Getty Images
Thanks to	Paul Cemmick

BBC Books, an imprint of Ebury Publishing, 20 Vauxhall Bridge Road, London SW1V 2SA.
BBC Books is part of the Penguin Random House group of companies whose addresses
can be found at global.penguinrandomhouse.com. Copyright © Match Of The Day magazine,
2015. First published by BBC Books in 2016. www.eburypublishing.co.uk. A CIP catalogue
record for this book is available from the British Library. ISBN 9781849909785
Commissioning editor: Albert DePetrillo; project editor: Grace Paul; production: Phil Spencer.
Printed and bound in Italy by Rotolito Lombarda SpA. Penguin Random House is committed
to a sustainable future for our business, our readers and our planet. This book is made from
Forest Stewardship Council ® certified paper.

5 headlines YOU want to read in 2017!

Here's your chance to not only become a headline writer but to also predict the future!

BURSTS AFTER BEAN BINGE

TOP SCIENTISTS were left gobsmacked yesterday when Premier League footballer .... **exploded after eating 88 tins of baked beans.**

The geeky lab boffins, who were called to the scene of the explosion by puzzled paramedics, could only scratch their heads in disbelief at what they called a "truly unique physiological event".

.... 's mum sobbed: "He loved beans, especially baked ones. It's how he would have wanted to go!"

ALIENS ABDUCT

....

FOOTBALL fans watched on in horror yesterday after superstar striker

.... **was smuggled aboard a UFO – before returning to Earth speaking alien.**

.... 's abduction, which was broadcast live on 24-hour news channels, lasted for an hour before he was beamed back to Earth covered in green slime, wearing a novelty sombrero and unable to speak English.

He said: "Plickle ma lickle tickle tickle, bo flozzle ma bozzle, slup!"

Children
should be
seen
and not
heard.

If you
can't be
good,
be
careful.

What's done
cannot be
undone.

R.I.P.

Dedicated to
Helen Mackenzie Smith
and to cat lovers everywhere.

Published in
Great Britain by
Jonathan Cape,
an imprint of Random House
Children's Books
A Random House Group
Company

JIM
A JONATHAN CAPE BOOK
978 0 224 08367 6

THIS EDITION
PUBLISHED
2009
All rights reserved

RANDOM HOUSE
CHILDREN'S
BOOKS
61-63 Uxbridge Road
London W5 5SA

Illustrations
copyright
© Mini Grey,
2009

Text copyright
© The Estate of
Hilaire Belloc,
1907, 2009

The right of Hilaire Belloc and Mini Grey to
be identified as the author and illustrator of this
work has been asserted in accordance with the
Copyright, Design and Patents Act 1988

www.kidsatrandomhouse.co.uk
www.rbooks.co.uk

Addresses for companies
within the Random House
Group Limited
can be found at:
www.randomhouse.co.uk/offices.htm

A CIP catalogue
record for this book is
available from
the British Library.
Printed and bound in
China

THE
RANDOM HOUSE
GROUP
Limited Reg. No. 954009